Praise for *Building Your Money Machine*

"Practical, rational, and real-world experience is brought to
life in *Building Your Money Machine*. Mel has a heart
of gold, and he brings it to each and every page."

— *David Bach, 10-time* New York Times *best-selling author
of* The Automatic Millionaire *and* The Latte Factor

"An insightful read that gives many lessons from a road well
traveled by a true money mentor who has run the miles himself."

— *Amy Porterfield, author of* The New York
Times *bestseller* Two Weeks Notice

"In a world full of confusing financial advice, *Building
Your Money Machine* is a clear, accessible guide to
achieving financial freedom. A must-read for anyone
who wants to take control of their financial future."

— *Farnoosh Torabi, host of the* So Money *podcast
and author of* A Healthy State of Panic

"Mel is my go-to guy when it comes to all things finance.
Delaying your financial future is easy, but Mel literally
gives you the map and frameworks to start now. The
approach is so straightforward that anyone can grasp it."

— *Stacy Tuschl, founder of Well-Oiled Operations*

"Finally a book that provides the direction and path to financial
freedom. Choose to take the path. Choose to take *action*. Choose to
allow Mel's unparalleled track record to drive *your* financial *success*."

— *Ben Newman, two-time* Wall Street Journal
best-selling author of Uncommon Leadership *and*
USA Today *Top 5 Mindset & Performance Coach*

"This is for anyone looking to escape the rat race and live life on their own terms. It is a whole new way of thinking about money, financial freedom, and how to make it your reality."

— *Jenna Kutcher*, *host of the* Goal Digger *podcast and* New York Times *best-selling author of* How Are You, Really?

"An empowering money resource with practical, actionable tips and strategies. If you want to take charge of your money story and rewrite your financial future, this book is a must-read."

— *Rick Mulready*, *founder of* The Art of Online Business *podcast and seven-figure business owner*

"Mel uses his gift of storytelling and his ability to create frameworks that visually offer a simple path to wealth building. This book is jam-packed with lessons, life experiences, and opportunities for transformation!"

— *Jessica Glazer DeRose*, *entrepreneur*

"This book is 100 percent a calling. Not only is this now mandatory reading for my 1:1 clients, but more importantly, it became a mandatory read for my daughters, ages 13 and 15."

— *Rachel Luna*, *certified master coach and a* Forbes-*rated* Top 11 Inspiring Female Entrepreneur

"Mel's use of storytelling, outlining of processes, and development of frameworks makes *Building Your Money Machine* unlike anything you have ever read. It is real, is actionable, and it is life changing."

— *Pat Flynn*, *best-selling author of* Will It Fly? *and* Superfans

"A timeless creation that will guide you to the financial freedom you deserve. Your future self will thank you for acting on Mel's brilliant wisdom."

— *Trent Shelton*, *best-selling author of* The Greatest You *and* Protect Your Peace *and motivational speaker*

"*Building Your Money Machine* is an insightful read that gives a lifetime of practical experience from a true money mentor. A life-changing manual for anyone seeking control over their financial destiny, without needing to make years of wrong turns to arrive there."

— *Matthew Hussey*, New York Times *best-selling author of* Love Life *and host of* Love Life with Matthew Hussey

"Mel does a masterful job of taking complex financial concepts and breaking them down into simple checklists, visual frameworks, and actionable advice. This is one of the best books on money I've ever read!"

— *Rory Vaden*, *co-founder of Brand Builders Group and* New York Times *best-selling author of* Take the Stairs

"This is not just a book; it's a golden ticket to a life of freedom, choice, and financial security. Prepare to see your life and finances in a whole new light!"

— *Glo Atanmo*, *serial entrepreneur and founder of The Life Leap*

"Mel is my go-to financial growth guru. I trust his insights knowledge, and his ability to make intimidating concepts feel attainable and freeing. This book is no different. Love his brilliant brain, but love his heart for helping people more."

— *Jasmine Star*, *CEO, podcast host, and motivational speaker*

"Abundance is your birthright. In *Building Your Money Machine* Mel shares a practical blueprint to financial empowerment and fulfillment."

— **Koya Webb**, *wellness entrepreneur and author of* Let Your Fears Make You Fierce

"A transformative guide that illuminates the path to financial freedom and empowers you to achieve your dreams!"

— **Lindsey Schwartz**, *founder of Powerhouse Women*

"The world doesn't function on good intentions, it functions on money. You need to understand it and create your own machine to safeguard yourself and your family's dreams for now and the future. This book is the greatest tool and strategy to do so. If you want financial freedom and a free life, you need to get this book."

— **Anthony Trucks**, *former NFL athlete and founder of Dark Work*

"With his unparalleled insights into wealth, investing, and finance, Mel has unlocked the secrets to financial success."

— **James Wedmore**, *founder of Business by Design and host of* Mind Your Business

"This is a whole new way of thinking about money, financial freedom, and how to finally make it a reality in your life. It's time to get your money working for you, and time to let Mel show you how to do it right."

— **Niyc Pidgeon**, *award-winning positive psychologist, business mentor, and best-selling author of* Now Is Your Chance

"Mel lays out an easy-to-follow, real-life path
to becoming financially free that doesn't force
you to go to extremes in order to achieve it!"

— **Chris Harder**, *founder of Frello,*
philanthropist, and investor

"Building Your Money Machine not only teaches you how to
optimize your assets and time but also inspires you to live
intentionally. A revolutionary approach to personal finance!"

— **Randy Garn**, New York Times *best-selling author*
of Prosper *and co-founder of Prosper Inc.*

"A brilliant balance of practical frameworks
and relatable stories that'll help you take control
of your financial destiny once and for all."

— **Natasha Willis**, *co-founder of School of Bots*

"This is a *must-read* for anyone who is tired of the 'skip-the-five-
dollar-coffee-and-save-every-dollar' advice and wants a clear path
to financial freedom based on *you* and the lifestyle *you* want."

— **Brandon Lucero**, *entrepreneur and host of The*
New Generation Entrepreneur Podcast

"Mel's use of frameworks and stories bridges the gap
between aspiration and action. *Building Your Money Machine*
is a simple and understandable recipe for living a rich life."

— **Shannon Weinstein, CPA**, *founder*
of Keep What You Earn®

"Few people can take an overwhelming topic such as money and make it as exciting, empowering, and actionable as Mel can. A must-read if you are someone who wants to create more abundance in your life than you ever thought possible and finally live the life of your dreams."

— *Kathrin Zenkina*, *manifestation expert, founder of Manifestation Babe©, and host of the top-rated show* The Manifestation Babe Podcast

"Real insights from a real student of the game. Mel is committed to helping others learn how to build their money machine on the road to financial freedom."

— *Jason Brown*, *stock market coach/options trader and founder of The Brown Report*

"A life-changing book that will show you how to create true financial freedom!"

— *Selena Soo*, *seven-figure business mentor and publicity expert*

BUILDING *your* MONEY MACHINE

BUILDING *your* MONEY MACHINE

HOW TO GET YOUR MONEY TO WORK HARDER FOR YOU THAN YOU DID FOR IT!

MEL H. ABRAHAM, CPA

HAY HOUSE LLC

Carlsbad, California • New York City
London • Sydney • New Delhi

Published in the United States by: Hay House LLC: www.hayhouse.com®
Published in Australia by: Hay House Australia Publishing Pty Ltd: www
.hayhouse.com.au • *Published in the United Kingdom by:* Hay House UK Ltd:
www.hayhouse.co.uk • *Published in India by:* Hay House Publishers (India)
Pvt Ltd: www.hayhouse.co.in

Cover design: Kostis Pavlou
Interior design: Joe Bernier
Interior photos/illustrations: Mel H. Abraham

Cataloging-in-Publication Data is on file at the Library of Congress

Hardcover ISBN: 978-1-4019-7950-8
E-book ISBN: 978-1-4019-7951-5
Audiobook ISBN: 978-1-4019-7952-2

10 9 8 7 6 5 4 3 2 1
1st edition, June 2024

Printed in the United States of America

SUSTAINABLE
FORESTRY
INITIATIVE

Certified Chain of Custody
Promoting Sustainable Forestry
www.forests.org
SFI-01268

SFI label applies to the text stock

This product uses responsibly sourced papers and/or recycled materials. For more information, see www.hayhouse.com.

This book is dedicated to my dad, Joseph Abraham, who stood quiet but strong and loved us with everything he had. Dad, you were the inflection point for our whole existence. Without the courageous choices you made, I would not be here, and the rest would all be gone too. You showed me that "because it was the right thing to do" is the way to live life. And you are the epitome of living a life that outlives you, because you are still living within the pages of this book and within me, Jeremy, and your great-grandchildren. Thank you for being one of the greatest men in my life.

CONTENTS

PART IV: LIVE THE JOURNEY

DISCLAIMER

Professional Advice and Limitations

The information and strategies provided in this personal finance book are intended for general educational and informational purposes only. While the author is a certified public accountant (CPA), the content of this book does not create a CPA/advisor–client relationship between the author and the reader. The author is not acting as your CPA, financial advisor, or attorney.

The author is not an attorney, and the information provided in this book should not be considered legal advice. Laws and regulations governing personal finance, taxation, and other related matters vary from country to country and state to state. As such, the information contained in this book may not be applicable or suitable for your specific situation, and you should not rely solely on the information presented in this book for making financial decisions or implementing financial strategies.

It is highly recommended that you consult with a qualified professional, such as a CPA, financial advisor, or attorney, who is familiar with your unique circumstances and the specific laws and regulations applicable to your country or state. These professionals can provide individualized guidance and advice tailored to your personal financial situation and goals.

By using the information in this book, you agree that the author and publisher are not responsible for any errors or omissions, or for any actions you take based on the information provided. The author and publisher expressly disclaim any liability for any losses, damages, or other consequences that may arise from you taking actions based on information within this book without seeking personal advice or the proper guidance that considers your particular situation or circumstances.

FOREWORD

In the dynamic landscape of entrepreneurial success and personal growth, Mel Abraham's *Building Your Money Machine* provides a clear path grounded in authenticity and practical strategy. This isn't just a book; it's a revolution in understanding the true essence of wealth creation and legacy building.

What I resonate most deeply with is that Mel doesn't just talk money—he talks life. His holistic approach is a breath of fresh air, proving that financial prosperity isn't the goal but the means to a life with choices, freedom, and opportunities. He democratizes financial freedom, showing us it's not just a dream for the elite but an achievable reality for everyone willing to take thoughtful, intentional steps. His Wealth Priority Ladder™ isn't just a tool; it's a life-changer, offering a step-by-step guide to not just financial security but abundance.

If you're someone like me who really values a clear road map, you'll love that what sets *Building Your Money Machine* apart is its journey-like structure. It takes you from the basics of understanding your financial stance to the nitty-gritty of creating a self-sustaining, robust financial ecosystem. Mel's expertise is layered with genuine emotional intelligence, the kind only someone who's been through the financial wringer and come out stronger could impart.

This book is more than a money manual; it's a reflection and acknowledgment of your untapped potential. Mel's personal stories bring a much-needed human touch and lightness to the world of finance. These stories remind us that the road to success is imperfect and will never look linear, even though you're taking steps forward.

In today's world, where financial literacy is so crucial yet often sidelined, *Building Your Money Machine* is an essential tool. It's a call to action for anyone looking to not just build wealth and personal freedom but to use it with purpose, integrity, and generosity.

Mel's vision goes beyond personal gain; it's about the legacy you create for your family, community, and future generations.

Reflecting on Mel's profound insights, it's clear this book is more than educational—it's transformative. It challenges you to rethink your financial beliefs and your vision of what's possible, and step up as the architect of your future.

Honestly, this is the book we've all been waiting for—it's the key to unlocking financial freedom and embracing a life of profound meaning and richness. I hope it leaves a lasting imprint on you like it did me and helps you build a future that looks far happier, healthier, and wealthier than your past.

— **Natalie Ellis**, founder and CEO of BossBabe

The people who get on in this world are the people who get up and look for the circumstances they want, and, if they can't find them, make them.

— GEORGE BERNARD SHAW

INTRODUCTION

I sat on the bay windowsill, watching him as he said, "We simply can't afford it." It was the first time I ever saw him crying. This was a man that was the tower of power to me as a five-year-old. He was the fixer, the solver, and the caretaker to so many, but on this day he stood in tears, looking at my mom and saying: "I'm trying to give you and the family everything you want. Working hard and doing what I think I'm supposed to do. But I feel like I'm a disappointment and letting you down. That's the very last thing I ever want to do—disappoint the ones I love the most."

I'm not sure that at five years old I had any clue of what was happening, but what I did know was it had to do with money. It looked like my dad was being crushed by the burden of his expectations and his desire to be more in the eyes of the ones he loved the most.

I wonder how often we feel this kind of weight from our own finances. In a recent study, the American Psychological Association found that 66 percent of people say that finances is one of their biggest stressors.[1] That is a travesty and needs to change.

My father was a hardworking, quiet man who always wanted to do what was right and take care of the people he loved. His single ambition was to provide for his family and give us a better life than he had growing up. He was raised in Iraq during a time of great persecution, risking his life to protect his family and others before he finally escaped to the United States to go to school and make a life. He always lived his life by the motto "It's the right thing to do." So you can imagine thinking that he was letting those he loved down would have hit him hard . . . and it did.

I started my own entrepreneurial journey at the age of 11, doing magic shows for kids' birthdays. Once I saw that I could make money doing what I loved while impacting people, I was hooked. Fast-forward a couple more decades: I had just embarked on a new entrepreneurial journey after an 11-year stint as a CPA. My partners had left me with $300,000 in debt, no cash, no business, and no clients. That year, my son, Jeremy, came to live with me, and I became a full-time single dad. Coincidentally, Jeremy was 5 years old at the time, and I was 34—nearly the same age my dad had been during that fateful memory when I saw him cry for the first time.

I was terrified. How could I possibly take care of this child? Fatherhood was a huge responsibility, and I felt clueless, but I knew I wanted to make sure I did right by Jeremy and that he was cared for and felt safe. I didn't want to let Jeremy down.

Fueled by fear and a desire to give Jeremy everything I could, I did what most loving parents and entrepreneurs do: I dug in, put my head down, and worked tirelessly. I was running, running, running, giving everything my all, believing every single invest-ment of my time and energy was to provide everything we could ever need or want in this life. Soon I found clients and started building my business, and gradually, success followed. As the cash began to flow, I thought I was doing well, both for myself and for Jeremy. I said to myself, *Look! We did it! We made it!* It was finally all coming together. So I kept running, running, running.

One day, Jeremy came home from school and rushed in to see me, like an excited child on their birthday morning. "Daddy, Daddy! I drew a picture of you at school today!"

I stopped working to kneel down and take the drawing from his hand, curious about what he'd created. What I saw stunned me . . .

. . . a blue stick figure glued to two computer screens, with a phone in each ear and another ringing on the desk. It was as if Jeremy were holding up a mirror and saying, "This is you. This is how I see you, and this is who you are."

Jeremy's drawing was a wake-up call. I had been doing what many of us are used to: working nonstop because we believe that's the only way to fulfill the expectations of life. I was so fixated on money and providing for my family that I had lost sight of what truly mattered—being present and spending quality time with my loved ones. It would have been easy for me to justify working so hard. I could have shaken off my son's drawing of me and explained, "But, kid, this is for us. I've got to be on the phone, on the computer, to do all these things so we can have the roof over our heads, so we can go to Disneyland, so we can do things we want to do."

But the fact was, no matter how much I tried to get him to understand why we needed the profits, he didn't want my profits. He wanted my presence. In *his* mind, it wasn't him and me having fun—no Disneyland, no playing ball. It was simply me, working. No matter how I tried to spin it, I was letting Jeremy down, and I then felt what my dad had felt decades earlier.

Everyone around me told me I needed to find work-life balance. But "balance" insinuates that you're managing two opposing forces, offsetting them to reach balance in a sort of tug-of-war. That doesn't work! There's no such thing as work-life balance. You cannot live in a work bucket for eight to ten hours, then come home to jump in a life bucket or a hobby bucket. Life isn't meant to be compartmentalized or disjointed like that. Doing things that way only leads to conflict, friction, and stress.

You see, I realized it actually isn't work-life balance we need; it is *work-life harmony.*

Harmony is a result of being intentional with how you live your life. Too often we find ourselves living a life that isn't of our own design but the design of societal, parenting, social media, or career expectations.

Jeremy's drawing was the catalyst for me to find a different way to do business, life, and money—a way where I could be intentional, be in harmony, and serve the greatest gift that I had been given at the time: being a father. It was the beginning of a transformative journey, one that allowed me to achieve peace by restructuring my business to align with my values and build wealth that would harmonize with all areas of my life—and help others achieve it too.

Let's face it, many of us have a story or narrative tied to money that shapes our beliefs about earning, saving, and spending it. Since most of us grew up in an environment where we never talked about money (and were never taught how to think about money), whatever we knew about money we learned through observation of those around us, the media, and now social media. We were left to our own devices to develop our own understanding and meaning for the stories we told ourselves around money, wealth, and financial freedom. I was no different, and it took me making a number of bad money decisions (which you'll hear more about later in this book) before I finally decided to search for the truth about money, my money stories, and how to take back control of my financial destiny.

Here's what I know: my dad thought he wasn't making enough money and that he was disappointing those he loved. Then Jeremy's drawing made me realize that even though I *was* making money, I was still disappointing someone I loved, because money wasn't what truly mattered to him. The reality is, these two events are what set in motion my financial journey to learn how to build a money machine that would multiply my income and allow my money to work harder for me than I ever had for it—so I would have complete control of the moments in my life to spend with those I love, doing things I love, and getting behind the causes I love.

This is when I realized that time is our greatest currency, not dollars, and in order to increase our true wealth, we need to be on two parallel journeys. The first journey is the Earning Journey, where the focus is on optimizing our value and the cash flow from that value. The result of this journey is to give a solution, have an impact, and generate cash flow. The second (and the one that is most often forgotten) is the Money Journey. This is where we are optimizing our assets and optimizing our time. This journey is where we find our freedom, legacy, and choice. We will look at both journeys here but delve more deeply into the Money Journey, since this is the one that most people are missing.

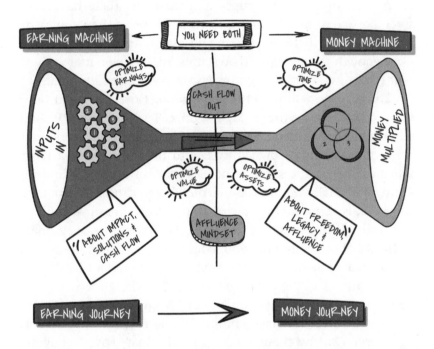

As much as this book is about money, it's about so much more. It's about how we show up and live our lives. There's a gap between how good we are and how good we are capable of being. This gap exists in many aspects of our lives, including our personal finances. Improving your financial situation may require sacrifice, change, or additional work, but remember that nobody is born a finance expert. Your financial journey is about making decisions that align with your goals and desires. It's not about deprivation; it's about intentionality. In the coming chapters, you'll learn simple, real-world lessons to make smarter choices with money, invest wisely, and protect your financial future.

Over more than three decades (yes, I am that old, LOL), I've developed and honed a process that has led to creating a Money Machine, my financial liberation, and helped countless others achieve the same. I'm thrilled to share this process with you because I know that it can transform your life in a remarkably short time. I'll share the money mistakes I've made so you can learn from my own screwups—and trust me, there have been some big screwups. Heck, I've lost more money than some will ever make in a lifetime, yet I'm still here. I'm fortunate to have done enough things right to be successful, but even more important is that I've done enough things wrong to be educational.

You get to benefit from the many wrong turns I've taken along the way without having to pay the price. The principles I'll share allowed me to bounce back in just 18 months from losing one-third of everything I owned (well into the millions) in a Ponzi scheme. They're the same principles that sustained me and my family financially when I was diagnosed with cancer. The point is this book is about taking care of your financial destiny and putting yourself in a position not to worry if you'll be okay financially. It's about equipping you, educating you, and empowering you to create the life you want, your way, and on your terms.

The principles I'm about to share with you are the same ones these people implemented: my son and his wife, who were able to own three homes and have a multimillion-dollar net worth before they turned 30; my client Bobbie, who eliminated over six figures of debt within 90 days; and my client Megan, who is working only four hours a day, four days per week, with plans to stop working six years from now by choice. They all had different backgrounds and circumstances and visions, but they're on track for the lives they want, because they're using the Money Machine principles.

I want to share this system with you so you too can find freedom and reclaim your time by building a Money Machine that works. By following the strategies and techniques outlined in this book, you'll learn how to create a Money Machine that generates income without your active efforts and allows you to enjoy financial freedom. This machine will give you the peace of mind that comes with knowing that you're truly free.

This book is part money philosophy, part money mindset, part strategy, and part tactical action. Just like I don't believe in passive income (we'll talk deeper about why passive income isn't the answer), I don't believe you can build the wealth and freedom you want without actively pursuing it.

This means doing stuff! And doing stuff you haven't done before—because let's face it, if you had, you'd already have the wealth. But hey, that's okay, because you're here and you have this book. You'll find sections where I ask you to reflect and write about your dreams and desires, because if your wealth isn't leading you directly to them, then why build it? That's exactly why we start with getting vividly clear on what those are, because I want you to live your dream as a reality, not just a daydream you never experience.

Now, as much reflection as there is in this book, there's also excavation of your current reality. The point is not to judge it but to understand it and springboard forward from it.

Over the next four parts, you'll have the chance to map your financial journey toward freedom and affluence. We'll start in Part I by giving you an understanding of what the journey is about, why it matters, and the keys to make it real in your life. By the end of Part I, you'll also have the tools to eliminate the things that hold most people back.

In Part II, you'll dig into what you want your future to look like. This is about designing your life and lifestyle and getting clear on where you are today, but more important, on the gap you need to bridge to make your vision a reality.

Once you're clear on your destination and where you're starting from, we'll get down to the tactical ways to build the Money Machine that will fund your dreams. In Part III, you'll learn what to do with each dollar and how to grow the money so it creates a wealth momentum that grows at an ever-accelerating rate.

And this leads to Part IV, where we dive deeper into how to live the affluent life you design while making sure the wealth and Money Machine you created is self-sustaining and will transcend time. It becomes the financial inflection point that changes the financial destiny for the generations to come, if you do it the right way.

To get the most out of this book, it's important that you approach it with intention and commitment. Here are some tips to help you maximize what you learn:

1. **Read every section carefully.** This book is designed to take you through a step-by-step process for building your Money Machine. Make sure you read every section in detail to fully understand each concept and how it fits into the bigger picture.

2. **Take notes.** As you read, take notes in a journal on key points, concepts, and action steps. This will help you retain the information better and also serve as a reference point for later.

3. **Take your time.** Building a Money Machine is not something that can be rushed. Take the time to fully absorb and implement each step before moving on to the next. Rushing through the process may lead to mistakes or missed opportunities.

4. **Complete each Action Item.** At various points, you will see this icon:

It signals actions you should take based on the content in the section before it. The icons will guide you through applying the various tactics and strategies in the book. Your journal will be handy for completing some of these.

5. **Utilize the extra resources.** In addition to the book, there's a special resource page at MoneyMachineResources.com where you'll find a deeper dive into various money, investing, and wealth topics touched on in the book. This will help you deepen your knowledge and accelerate your results. The easiest way to access the resources is with this QR code:

6. **Stay committed.** Building a Money Machine is a long-term process that requires commitment and persistence. Stay focused on your goals and keep working toward them, even when things get tough.

Now grab your journal to document your thoughts, visions, goals, and plans, and let's get started!

Part I

UNDERSTAND THE JOURNEY

Wealth is not his that has it, but his that enjoys it.

— BENJAMIN FRANKLIN

CHAPTER 1

THE JOURNEY OF FINANCIAL LIBERATION

*Let people get caught up in the tidal wave of
your dream and just come along for the ride.*

— MEL ABRAHAM

I stared out at the skyline in downtown Los Angeles. It was 10
o'clock on a Friday night, yet another Friday night when I was
working late in one of the tallest buildings in LA.

It was 1989 and my fifth year at one of the largest consult-
ing firms in the world. As I admired the lights of the city on the
horizon, I realized that my current journey wasn't one of my own
design. I felt a yearning and pulling at my soul that kept saying,
*There has to be something more! Something more impactful. Something
more fulfilling! This can't be the rest of my life.*

The reality was that I wasn't sure what "more" was at that
time, but as I turned back toward the office, I looked at Tom, the
partner I was working for, toiling over papers at his desk. Like
looking in a crystal ball, I saw my future if I stayed on this path.

The problem was that it wasn't a future by my design. My
education, my profession, and my career path had been built
on the expectations of others, from society to my parents. My
dad came to the United States when he was 17 years old with
no money and no connections, but he still managed to achieve

a successful career as an engineer, start a family, and build a comfortable life for us. I had a lot to live up to as the child of immigrants, and I'd already disappointed my parents' first expectations for me by not becoming a doctor and having lots of kids! And yet somehow I was still on a path toward a future that was being designed *for* me and not *by* me—somewhat like an arranged marriage.

More important, when I looked at Tom I didn't see joy, fun, or fulfillment. I'm not even sure I saw accomplishment. What I saw was stress, angst, and a constant need to do more. I saw a man that was overweight, had high blood pressure, and was likely within inches of a heart attack.

That was my future if I stayed on this path. That was the day I quit.

Have you ever felt stuck in a job you despise? Trapped by your finances, unable to afford the things you truly want in life, and constantly stressed about bills and debt? If so, you're not alone. Millions of people around the world are struggling with financial insecurity or at least uncertainty, and it's taking a toll on their mental health, relationships, and overall well-being.

I previously mentioned that more than 66 percent of people say finances is one of their biggest stressors. The same APA study found that more than 35 percent felt *significant* stress.[1] If money and finances are causing this kind of stress to so many, there's no way we can find ourselves on a path to mental or physical wellness until we find financial wellness.

Here's another stat to consider on the other side of the equation. The overwhelming majority (79 percent) of millionaires in the United States did not receive any inheritance from their parents or other family members. In fact, the majority of millionaires didn't even grow up around a lot of money. According to a survey called *The National Study of Millionaires* by Ramsey Solutions, eight out of ten millionaires come from families at or below middle-income level. Only 2 percent of millionaires surveyed said they came from an upper-income family.[2]

What does that mean for you? That financial security and, ultimately, freedom are possible, and they're within your reach, no matter your age or stage of life or your circumstances. Regardless of where you're at today, you *can* change your financial future. Sure, everyone's boulders will be different sizes and the steepness of the hill we're each pushing the boulder up may be different. But "different" doesn't mean it's impossible.

Financial freedom is your birthright! It's only a matter of doing what it takes to claim it.

Financial freedom: this term has echoed through the minds of countless individuals who have dreamed of a life unburdened by monetary concerns. It's a powerful aspiration, yet many people see it as a distant or even impossible goal. But what if I told you that financial freedom isn't just a luxury, it's a *must* for a life of true fulfillment?

Financial freedom is about more than just achieving wealth or being able to afford a luxurious lifestyle. It's about breaking free from the limiting beliefs and habits that keep us stuck in a cycle of financial struggle. It's about gaining the confidence and tools to take control of our finances and create a life of abundance and purpose. It's about making informed decisions and escaping from the constraints that prevent us from living our best lives. It's about gaining the peace of mind that comes from knowing that our financial needs are met, not just for today, but for the future as well.

It's about living a life built on *choice* instead of survival. Imagine waking up every day feeling empowered, with the resources to live the life you truly desire.

When we achieve financial freedom, we unlock the door to a life filled with endless possibilities. We can choose to spend our time pursuing our passions, deepening our relationships, and making a lasting impact on the world. We are no longer limited by the need to constantly work to make ends meet, and we can focus our energy on what truly matters.

The first step toward financial liberation is understanding the concept of ultimate luxury. Ultimate luxury is the ability to enjoy the best years of your life well before and into your golden years. This means bucking societal norms and avoiding the debt spiral that so many people find themselves trapped in. Ultimately, money is not taboo or greedy unless you make it that way. In this book, we'll focus on using your money for a purpose: creating a legacy and having a lasting impact.

To create a life of richness and fulfillment, you must avoid the trap of comparing yourself to others. The Joneses may appear to have it all, but appearances can be deceiving. It's important to define and design the life you want, whether that's living on a yacht in Monaco or camping in a tent in Montana. What matters is that the life you choose is right for you. If you're not in the financial position you want to be in today, that's okay. The key is to start where you are and make the necessary changes to move forward.

Achieving financial freedom provides us with a sense of security and resilience in the face of life's uncertainties. Unexpected events such as medical emergencies, job loss, or other unforeseen circumstances can quickly derail our financial stability if we're not prepared. Financial freedom equips us with the resources and skills to navigate these challenges and maintain a sense of security for ourselves and our loved ones.

The pursuit of financial freedom is a transformative journey that can have a profound impact on every aspect of our lives. It not only benefits us on a personal level, but it also allows us to make a more significant impact on the world around us. When we achieve financial freedom, we're in a better position to support the causes that are important to us, to help those in need, and to foster positive change in our communities and beyond. Whether it's through philanthropy, volunteering, or other forms of giving back, financial freedom provides us with the resources and opportunities to contribute to causes that align with our values and make a meaningful difference in the lives of others.

Achieving financial freedom empowers us to create a legacy that extends far beyond our own lives. We can pass on the values of financial responsibility, hard work, and generosity to future generations, ensuring that they too have the opportunity to lead fulfilling lives and make a positive impact on the world.

As we take control of our finances and work toward our goals, we develop new skills, gain confidence, and become better equipped to navigate the complexities of life. We learn the value of hard work, discipline, and perseverance, and we gain a greater appreciation for the things that truly matter. Gaining control over our finances will help us develop a deeper understanding of our values, priorities, and vision for the life we want to lead. This newfound self-awareness empowers us to make more intentional choices about how we spend our time, energy, and resources, ultimately leading to greater fulfillment and happiness.

Here's the truth: The path to financial freedom is not paved with get-rich-quick schemes or the pursuit of material wealth. Achieving financial freedom is not an easy feat. It requires dedication, discipline, and a willingness to confront our fears and step outside of our comfort zones. It requires us to take risks, learn from our mistakes, and continually invest in ourselves and our future. But the rewards of this journey are immeasurable.

As we work toward financial freedom by building what I call a Money Machine, we must remember that it is not merely a destination to be reached but a lifelong pursuit that shapes the course of our lives and who we are. It is a journey that challenges us, inspires us, and ultimately empowers us to live our lives to the fullest. By embracing the pursuit of financial freedom, we create a life that is rich in every sense of the word, and we leave behind a legacy of abundance, impact, and inspiration for generations to come.

So, why should you strive for financial freedom? Because you deserve it. You deserve to live a life free from the stress and insecurity that comes with financial struggle. You deserve to pursue your passions and make a positive impact on the world. And most important, you deserve to be happy, healthy, and fulfilled.

MAXIMS TO REMEMBER TO GUIDE YOUR JOURNEY

Below are the maxims to remember on your journey. Bookmark this page and if you're ever unsure about where to go, reread these to keep you motivated.

Financial Freedom Unlocks the Potential of Your Life

Imagine waking up each day with a sense of calm, knowing your financial needs are met—not just for today but for the foreseeable future. The stress and anxiety that so often accompany money matters simply vanish, leaving room for a more profound connection to the things that truly matter in life—your passions, your relationships, your dreams, and your purpose.

Financial freedom unlocks the potential of your life, allowing you to pursue the experiences and opportunities that align with your values and aspirations. It gives you the power to say yes to the things that bring joy and meaning, and no to those that don't. It enables you to focus on creating a legacy and making a positive impact on the world rather than being consumed by the perpetual chase for material wealth.

Financial Freedom Is about More Than Just Money

Financial freedom is not about accumulating vast sums of money or living a life of extravagance. It's about gaining control over your financial destiny and breaking free from the chains of debt and the treadmill of living paycheck to paycheck. It's about creating a financial foundation that empowers you to live life on your terms, to choose your path, and to thrive in your purpose.

The journey toward financial freedom requires a shift in mindset and a willingness to embrace new ways of thinking and acting that foster long-term financial health. It's about cultivating financial literacy, developing effective money-management habits, and making informed decisions that align with your values and goals. It's about recognizing the importance of investing in yourself, your relationships, and your future.

The Pursuit of Financial Freedom Is a Catalyst for Personal Growth and Transformation

Embracing the pursuit of financial freedom can act as a powerful catalyst for personal growth and transformation. As you learn to manage your finances with intention and purpose, you will naturally develop a deeper understanding of your values, your priorities, and your vision for the life you want to lead. The skills and knowledge you gain will not only benefit your financial well-being but will also enhance your ability to navigate the many complexities of life with greater confidence and resilience.

Financial freedom fosters a sense of empowerment and self-reliance that extends far beyond the realm of money. It enables you to cultivate healthier relationships, explore new passions and interests, and create a life that is truly aligned with your values and aspirations. In the pursuit of financial freedom, you'll discover the courage to face your fears, to take risks, and to embrace the extraordinary potential that lies within you.

Financial Security Is a Moral Imperative

I firmly believe that the pursuit of financial freedom is not just a personal aspiration but a moral imperative. In a world where so many struggle with financial insecurity and the stress it brings, we have a responsibility to ourselves, our families, and our communities to prioritize financial well-being. By empowering ourselves with the knowledge and skills necessary to achieve financial freedom, we can create a ripple effect that benefits not only our own lives but those of others around us.

In pursuing financial freedom, we demonstrate to our children the importance of financial literacy, responsible money management, and the ability to be financially independent and self-sufficient members of society who have the ability to be more generous with time and money. We model the behaviors and values that will enable them to build a strong financial foundation and to make wise decisions throughout their lives. By investing in our own financial well-being, we create a more stable and secure future for ourselves and for generations to come.

Moreover, financial freedom allows us to make a more significant impact in our communities and the world at large. With a solid financial foundation, we can contribute to causes that align with our values, support those in need, and foster positive change on a broader scale. Financial freedom is not just about personal enrichment; it's about creating a world where everyone has the opportunity to thrive.

We Can Design Our Own Future and a Life Worth Living

In the pursuit of financial freedom, we embark on a journey that enriches every aspect of our lives. We learn to appreciate the true value of our time, our relationships, and our experiences rather than measuring our worth by the size of our bank accounts or the material possessions we own.

By embracing the pursuit of financial freedom, we create a life worth living—one filled with purpose, passion, and the freedom to choose our own path. It's a life that allows us to focus on the things that truly matter and to leave a lasting legacy that reflects our values, our dreams, and our aspirations.

In the pages of this book, I will share with you the tactics, strategies, mindset shifts, and frameworks you need to achieve financial freedom that have worked for me and others throughout time, not some flash-in-the-pan fads. I will guide you on a journey toward greater freedom, prosperity, and abundance. And I'll show you that no matter where you are on your financial journey, you have the power to create the life you truly want. I want to help you create a life that outlives you.

BUILDING A MONEY MACHINE IS IMPERATIVE FOR YOUR FREEDOM

It was a sunny day in 2019, and I was reflecting on my life while flying back home to Southern California after masterminding with some of the top entrepreneurs of our time. I was feeling good. I had just completed an amazing mid-six-figure launch. I was traveling and speaking on some of the biggest stages around. As I stepped off the private G5 jet I was flying on, I was excited to see my wife, Stefanie, in our home on the sand in Laguna Beach. We truly felt we were living our best lives.

But life can change in a moment. Two weeks after stepping off that plane, I found myself in a hospital bed, listening to words I thought I would never hear.

"You have cancer."

I was in shock. *How could this be?* I never smoked, barely drank, ate healthy (okay, I had a sweet tooth), and worked out five or six days a week. No one in my family had ever had cancer. But suddenly, my whole existence was in jeopardy.

"We found a seven-and-a-half-centimeter tumor in your bladder. It's on top of the prostate, which means we may have to remove the prostate. We can't see the ureter on the right side, which means we may have to put a tube and a bag in for the kidney, and if it's really bad, we may have to remove your bladder."

Wait! What? What is life like without a bladder?

I was facing the fight of my life, because I wanted to live and I knew I wasn't ready to go. I loved my life and my people too much.

I'm not going to lie to you; I was scared. Actually, I was petrified about what this journey was going to be like. I was diagnosed on a Friday, and Stefanie and I lay in bed all day Saturday, crying until we had no tears left. Sunday, I finally realized I could either live in denial or accept my current circumstance and fight the good fight—and fight is what we did.

We put together a team of doctors, but even after multiple tests, we couldn't figure out how I got cancer. It was hard to accept that the rest of my life had to go on hold until more was known.

But I had a luxury that not everyone has: financial freedom. When my son, Jeremy, gave me his workaholic-dad picture 23 years before, I realized I had to do business and money differently. I realized that having a business or a job was not where I would find freedom, control, and choice. The freedom I actually wanted in my life would be found through making an impact and creating cash flow, which could then be used to build a machine—a Money Machine.

I knew I would have to fight the cancer medically, physically, psychologically, and spiritually and face all the stress and uncertainty that went along with it. But because of my Money Machine, I didn't have to fight the cancer *financially*.

I didn't have to question which doctors to go to, if I could afford the treatments, or if I could take time away from my job. I had the luxury, privilege, and blessing of not having to worry about working through the days and fighting for my life at the same time. Even though I hadn't known I was going to get cancer, because of how I'd structured everything, I was able to shut down the business and step away. I had a machine that was going to give me money so I could focus on healing. I could focus on the fight. I could spend each day, every day, all day going to the doctors, working on the treatments, trying all the alternatives; doing all the Western medicine, the Eastern medicine, even the far-out medicine—everything to fight the cancer and make sure that I could stay here with my family, the people I love to experience life with. Earning money did not have to cross my mind.

When I was diagnosed with cancer, I struggled to work out why I got it. *What did I do to deserve it? What did I do wrong?* I wanted so much to find someone or something to blame. I think we all do this when we're dealt unexpected circumstances. But all that did was spiral me into resentment, anger, and despair—until I looked at it differently. I'd been searching the past to find a reason for the cancer until it dawned on me . . . *What if the reason isn't in the past? What if it's in the future?*

If it was in the future, then I once again had a choice: I could decide what *I* wanted to make the cancer mean.

So maybe, just maybe, the reason I was given cancer was to raise my awareness to the fact that many people are struggling financially who don't need to. . . . To open up the conversations about money, building wealth, or the incredible gift of financial freedom. . . . To light the path to make it a reality no matter your age or stage, and to help you build this Money Machine that provides for you the way it did for me.

The Money Machine is about getting your money to work harder for you than you did for it. You can do this by following the process I outline in this book to increase the money you make and keep more of it at the same time. Then, by following a very specific allocation process for what to do with the money and investing the money consistently over time, you literally build your Money Machine. The investments that make up the Money Machine will continue to grow until it comes to a point where it can act as your ATM. You can take money out when you need it for emergencies or pay for the vacations you always wanted to take or support those causes that matter to you.

I'll dig deeper into exactly how it works and what you need to do to make it a reality, but know that this is the key to your financial freedom.

Before we build the machine, let's first address the foundation: the right mindset.

CHAPTER 2

OVERCOMING EXCUSES TO UNLOCK WEALTH CREATION

*Just because it's unfamiliar doesn't
mean it's risky or complicated.*

— MEL ABRAHAM

The reality is that no one has money issues.

I know you might sit back and say, "Oh, you haven't seen *my* bank account. You haven't seen my life." You're right, I haven't, but I have seen a lot of people's lives, including my own. No one has money issues. What we really have are money *symptoms*. These money symptoms are a result of the choices, behaviors, and decisions we've made in the past.

Now, I get it—accepting that our current financial state is a result of the choices, behaviors, and decisions we've made in the past can be confronting because it can feel a lot like blame. Yet it should be empowering to know that if all you did was change some choices, behaviors, and habits, your whole money situation would change. You see, it's not about blame at all. It's about understanding your ability to take control of your situation. Control the controllables, and prepare for the uncontrollables the best you can.

So, what typically stands in the way of good money behaviors, habits, and decisions? It's the stories we tell ourselves, the beliefs we have, and the excuses we make. By removing these, we clear the path for better money behaviors and habits to unlock our wealth creation.

CONFRONTING OUR MONEY STORIES

As someone who has worked with more than 100 millionaires and billionaires to help them navigate their money, wealth, and life transitions along the way, I can attest to the fact that everyone struggles with some degree of guilt and shame around money. It doesn't matter where they are in life; they all have stories that hold them back and stir a little trepidation or fear. When I first came into this space to start teaching, my background was as an accountant. In accounting, we do numbers, columns, and rows, and everything adds up and it's beautiful. So originally, I thought I would simply teach tactics and just give these people the tools and the frameworks to get the job done. It didn't take me long to figure out that if we don't deal with the stuff in our minds, we'll never deal with the stuff in the bank accounts. (Read that again.) If we don't address the stories we tell ourselves about money, we will never achieve the wealth we desire or deserve.

In Part III, when we discuss the gap (the place between where you are today and where you want to be), I'm going to walk you through the Habit Builder™ framework to show how to change your habits and behaviors so you can actually get the results you want instead of the results you currently have. This is the exact four-part framework I take my Elite clients through, no matter whether they have $100, $100,000, or millions and beyond, because of the results it produces. The Habit Builder will allow you to take control of your financial future and prove that the biggest difference between where you are today and where you want to be comes down to your behaviors, choices, and habits.

But first, we need to understand how and why the money stories we create can make such an impact on our lives from a financial standpoint. The fact is, we never get any formal education around money, wealth, or just finances in general. Only 14 states in the U.S. require high schoolers to take a course on money, which is a travesty. We need more schools to require this. It should be a core skill that we teach our youth.

Further, because we're told not to talk about money, money becomes a source of tension rather than a tool to bring us closer. But if we learn to have safe conversations about money, reframe our narrative, and view money as a means to support causes, help others, and make a positive impact, we open ourselves up to abundance and success.

Unfortunately, since money is not intentionally taught to us and we're not having open and safe conversations about it, most of what we learn is by watching what others do with their money. I often say that most money lessons are "caught, not taught." We catch our money lessons primarily through observation.

We've watched our parents, but most of them had no formal training or study and were often also struggling to figure out the money issues in their lives. We're watching on social media, even though we know people parade their facades of a perfect life that's not rooted in reality. It's easy to believe these so-called "influencers" without knowing the whole story. Many of them are likely buried in debt so they can create the facade. This is a materialistic show without a connection to the reality of how it was acquired. We observe what the media says, but the media is all about ratings and advertising, not truly informing and empowering.

So where and from whom are we getting our true financial wisdom?

The reality is, it's not the story that does this to us; rather, it's the meaning we give to the story. This is something I call the Money Story Dynamic™. The meaning you give your money stories is not in the facts of what happened but in how you interpreted the facts. And from that meaning we slowly craft our money identity, which then leads to our behavior. Well, how's that going to serve us down the road? Just look at what happened to me when I saw my dad and mom fight about money at five years old. I interpreted that single moment to mean that if I don't have enough money, I will disappoint people I love. But was that the truth?

Of course not. It was my interpretation of a moment that I then carried with me as if it *were* fact and truth—until Jeremy shined a light on it with his drawing.

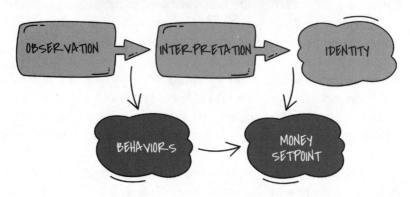

MONEY STORY DYNAMIC™

Think about it this way: If I see money as a greedy tool, or if I see money as dirty and bad, it's going to create a behavior in alignment with that identity and belief. And when it creates that behavior, it also creates what I call your Money Setpoint—a point that you'll never rise above until you remove those limitations. What you need to do in these cases is to look at your beliefs and separate the observation (the facts of what happened) from the interpretation that you gave it.

Here's what I know: 18 percent of people making over $100,000 per year are still living paycheck to paycheck.[1] And 35 percent of these folks could not pay for a $400 unexpected expense. What is more, 26 percent of adults have literally *nothing* saved for retirement.

But that stops now! You are not going to be a statistic. Not on my watch! That is, if you follow my principles.

THE TOP 6 EXCUSES KEEPING US STUCK IN OUR MONEY STORY

Think about this instead. What if you create a new story? "Money is something that allows me to get behind causes and missions, help charities, make a difference, and know that I'm helping people heal." That's an *entirely* different story and one that will make money show up in brand new and exciting ways in your life!

The fact is, we can have reasons or results. We can't have both. It's easy for people to say, "I don't have the ability to build wealth. I'm not making a lot. No one in my family has ever made a lot. My job doesn't pay well."

I get it. I remember when I was $300,000 in debt with no job or clients, and all the circumstances around me were saying how dire my situation looked. But I could either focus on the trees blocking my path or on creating the path through the trees. The tough-love truth is that the only things keeping us broke are excuses and the mistakes holding us back from the wealth we deserve.

So I want to take the time to identify the top six excuses I regularly hear and give the facts around them so we can move through them. It's important that you read through these and reflect whether any resonate with you. When we examine the mistakes and excuses that are keeping us stuck in the same patterns, time after time, year after year, we can solve the problem and move toward financial freedom. And as we move through them, you'll start to see how you can take faster and better control over your own financial world—so this is a crucial part of your journey.

Excuse #1: "I have plenty of time" or "I'm too late now."

Many people believe that they have plenty of time to start building wealth, or, on the other end of the spectrum, feel that it's too late for them to start. It's imperative to understand that time is your greatest lever when it comes to creating wealth, so the sooner you can start building it, the easier it will be to create the level of wealth that you need to be financially free.

"I'll do it someday. Why start now?" is the mentality for the 20- and 30-year-olds who think they have plenty of time. "I'll never catch up, so why start now?" is often the mentality of the

40-, 50-, or 60-year-olds. Either way, both groups are sitting in inaction and not moving toward the financial freedom they desire and deserve. But there's an inverse relationship between time and money. The more time you have, the less money you need. And the less time you have, the more money you'll need.

For instance, my granddaughter Emily just turned one year old, and we've already started saving for her: $25 per week for her first 20 years of life. The $20,000 that will accumulate by the time she's 20 will have turned into over $1.5 million when she's 65.

See, time will do all the heavy lifting.

If you happen to be in the "it's too late" mindset instead, let me show you there's no better time than now to start your financial freedom journey. One of the worst things you can say is, "Well, I don't have much for retirement, so why should I try?" There are only a few possible outcomes from that attitude: you could find yourself living on meager government funds or working well into your golden years or moving in with your kids and depending on their support, all while reducing the quality of life you're living. None of these sound appealing to me, and I doubt they sound appealing to you either. Hear me out: I'm not ridiculing or criticizing, but I want us to find the desire and courage to say, "I'll get in the game no matter how big, no matter how small. Even if I only get twenty percent of where I want to go, I'm twenty percent closer than I would have been if I didn't do anything at all." And your life will be 20 percent better than it would've been otherwise.

Once you understand that wealth creation works on a curve, the wealth-creation journey will really make sense to you. The Wealth Creation Curve™ starts out flat for a period of time, and you feel like you aren't moving or growing at all. This is what I call the Wealth Flatline. Everyone, no matter when they start, must go through the Wealth Flatline. But when you do, on the other side of the Wealth Flatline is the Wealth Acceleration Zone. This is the zone of beautiful euphoria where your money gains momentum and grows at accelerated, exponential rates.

What does that mean for you and your financial future?

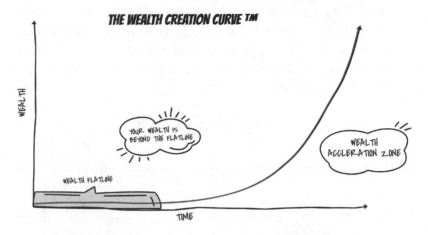

Don't give up—acceleration is coming. It won't happen overnight but over time. The biggest mistake is when people see no progress while in the Wealth Flatline and stop. Don't! Stay the course. Stay in the game, because everyone has to get through the Wealth Flatline. The sooner you start, the sooner you get to the other side.

Remember, building sustainable wealth is a long game, and it's built on your consistent behaviors, habits, and decisions. When you follow time-tested principles and road-tested processes, you'll get predictable results.

How about we land this plane by putting some numbers to it for you?

We'll look at what happens over time through the eyes of four different investors: Tom, Justin, Sally, and Angela.

- Tom is going to invest $5,000 a year from age 25 to age 35.

- Justin will also invest $5,000 a year, but he's going to start 10 years later, so from 35 to 45.

- Then we have Sally, who's going to start at the same age as Justin and invest $5,000 per year, but she's going to invest it from 35 all the way to 65.

- Finally we have Angela, who's also investing $5,000 per year, but she's going to start at age 25 and do it all the way up to 65.

Tom and Justin will both end up investing a total of $55,000. Sally is going to invest $150,000. Angela is going to invest $200,000.

Let's look at what happens by the age of 65 for each investor when using an 8 percent rate, which is conservative given the market's long-term returns.

THE POWER OF TIME

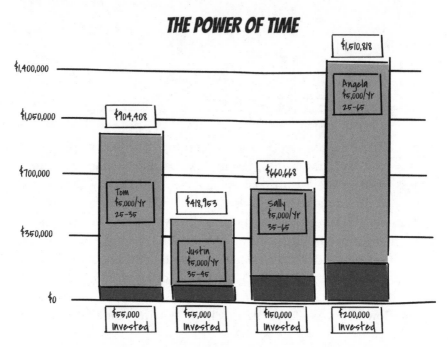

Remember, Justin and Tom invested the same amount of money for the same amount of time, but Justin started 10 years later than Tom. Because of that wait, Justin ended up with less than 50 percent of what Tom accumulated—time matters.

Now Sally, who started later and at the same time as Justin but kept it going longer, will get a little farther: to $660,000. That's 50 percent more than Justin, but she invested almost three times as much.

Then there's Angela, who started at the same time as Tom and stayed in the game for 40 years. She ends up with more than $1,500,000 dollars. Once again, time matters.

The fact of the matter is that for the best results, we should start early; if we didn't start early, we should start now. It's not the amount that matters as much as the time. It's not the amount that matters as much as the behavior.

Remember, when we start early, we're exercising and creating behaviors. When I started building financial habits with my son, Jeremy, he was 10 years old. He's now 33. Jeremy and his wife, Kamie, have three homes and a multimillion-dollar net worth, but they started small and let time do the work. When we get to Excuse #2, I'll explain what I did with Jeremy.

I've got other clients that started at 50 years old. Now they're 60, and in 10 years they've accumulated a million-dollar net worth because of how much they chose to invest.

If Jeremy had said, "I've got plenty of time, I'm going to wait," or if my clients had said, "It's too late to get started," none of them would be where they are today.

Excuse #2: "I need to make a lot of money" or "When I make more money, then I'll invest."

Many people believe that they need to make a lot of money to invest in wealth creation. The truth is that our ability to generate wealth is less about the amount and more about the behavior. Waiting until we make more money isn't an excuse that will serve us. It's going to put us further back and keep us behind the growth curve. We need to make wealth creation and investing a priority, and it will become part of our being through consistent behavior.

Also, the math doesn't lie. If we look at $200 per month over 30 years at 8 percent, it turns into over $300,000. That's just $200 a month, $50 a week, or less than $8 a day. What happens if we increase this to $800 per month? Boom: $1,200,000. My point is that it doesn't take a lot to make a lot. It simply takes the right behaviors consistently done over time.

You can do a side gig to bring the money in and put it away if you truly want that financial freedom. It's a matter of making some good money choices and decisions, and being very clear on your priorities in your life. We'll go deeper on this in Part II.

INCREMENTAL INCOME	NUMBER OF YEARS					
	5	10	15	20	25	30
$200	$14,793	$36,883	$69,669	$118,589	$191,473	$300,059
$500	$36,983	$92,083	$174,173	$296,474	$478,683	$750,148
$800	$59,173	$147,333	$278,676	$474,358	$765,893	$1,200,236
$1,200	$88,760	$220,999	$418,014	$711,537	$1,148,840	$1,800,354
$1,500	$110,950	$276,249	$522,518	$889,421	$1,436,050	$2,250,443

Assumes an 8% return

This is part of what I did with Jeremy. He was 10 years old when I started paying him $125 per month. From this, he took care of his school lunches and some other things as well as giving to charity, saving, and investing. It wasn't a lot, but it got him started early. It wasn't just about having more time for investments but more time for these behaviors to become ingrained habits—they became some of his weekly and monthly practices.

Our ability to generate wealth is less about the amount and more about the behavior.

Excuse #3: "I need to get out of debt first."

Many people believe that they need to get out of debt first before they start investing or building wealth. In fact, a number of money pundits espouse this—but not me. Building wealth is about developing the behavior and muscle of wealth creation, and so is debt management. But they are different muscles. I agree that if you totally focus on debt first, you will get out of debt faster, but then you haven't gotten into the Wealth Creation Curve, which means you'll be stuck in the Wealth Flatline longer. The other issue is that you're not building the wealth-creation muscles, so they're atrophying.

We need a balanced approach where we split our income in a way that works for us, to exercise the debt-management muscle while at the same time building the wealth-creation muscles.

We'll go deeper into exactly how to do this in Part III when we talk about the Wealth Priority Ladder.

Excuse #4: "I don't need to understand investing. My advisor takes care of it for me."

No one cares about and loves our financial future more than we do. We need to be the captain of our ship and make the choices, while our advisors are there to be servants to our vision. They help us navigate by giving us information and access to investments that are the best fit for us. The advisor must be doing things that are in our best interest, not their own.

Your advisor's job is, first off, to buy into your financial vision, or what I call an Affluence Vision™, that you'll build through doing the exercises in this book. They need to buy into that vision because you're going to build a plan to make that vision a reality. Their second job is to educate and inform you, to help you understand the decisions that you need to make and the investments that you may pursue. Don't invest in something you don't understand. If an advisor isn't willing to explain it to you, they're the wrong advisor. If they're not willing to spend whatever time it takes, they're the wrong advisor. If the investments they're putting in front of you are too complicated for where you're at, they're the wrong advisor.

It's why knowing what is going on with your financial situation is so important; it will help you know who can truly help you.

Be sure to read the Protect section of Part III to learn how to choose an advisor team that's right for you.

Excuse #5: "I'm not good enough or smart enough to do this."

Feeling not good or smart enough is probably the most common excuse that holds people back from achieving financial freedom. We all have limiting beliefs that hold us back, but we need to recognize that they're just beliefs, not facts. We need to challenge those beliefs and replace them with empowering ones that will serve us better.

Anyone can learn how to create wealth and invest in the stock market. It's not rocket science, but it does require some basic knowledge and discipline. The good news is that we can learn those skills through books (like the one already in your hands!), courses, and mentorship. We can also hire professionals to help us, like financial planners, accountants, and lawyers, but we still need to take ownership of our financial future and understand the decisions that we're making.

We also need to recognize that making mistakes is part of the learning process. No one is perfect, and we will make mistakes along the way. The key is to learn from those mistakes, adjust our plan, and keep moving forward.

Heck, I've lost repeatedly over the years with investments, bad decisions, and even outright fraud. But I'm still in the game and continuing to grow my wealth and myself. You can do the same, but the difference is, you don't need to make the same mistakes I made.

Excuse #6: "It's complicated, and I'm not good with numbers."

I get it, math isn't everyone's cup of tea. But when it comes to wealth building, all you need is some basic math. Your wealth is on the other side of that math.

The financial services industry wants us to feel that investing is complex, because it makes us dependent on them. But the real truth is that it's not complicated. Literally, if all you did was make money, spend less money than you make, and use the difference to invest on a consistent basis, your financial world would change. Investments can be simple. You can build a simple portfolio of index funds, and you don't even need an advisor for that.

Did any of these excuses hit home with you? If so, what could you do to shift your perspective to a more empowered place so you can be fully engaged in your financial freedom journey?

When you eliminate these excuses, you'll see a whole new trajectory for your wealth and your financial destiny.

THE WEALTH DRIVER MATRIX FOR CREATING MONEY MOMENTUM

When we examine the lives of individuals who have amassed wealth, we find commonalities that provide us with a road map to approach wealth creation. By understanding and implementing these common threads, we too can achieve financial freedom. Remember the Ramsey Solutions survey I mentioned in Chapter 1 that revealed that 79 percent of millionaires are first-generation millionaires?[2] The same survey showed that 31 percent of these millionaires built their wealth with an average annual income of $100,000 over their career, and one-third never made six figures in a single working year.[3] The fact that such a large percentage of millionaires have built their wealth from scratch shows that financial freedom is attainable for anyone willing to adopt the right mindset and habits.

In fact, there are only four things that drive your wealth. This is what I call the Wealth Drivers Matrix™. It consists of four key factors: *income, savings rate, investment returns,* and *time*. By understanding and controlling these factors, you can create Money Momentum, an acceleration of wealth that results from consistent, effective habits and behaviors.

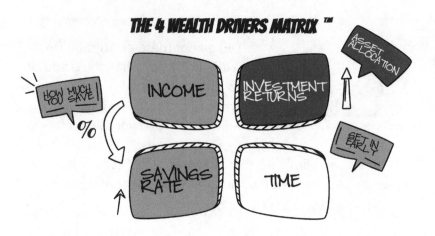

Driver #1: Income

Income, the first Wealth Driver, is a vital part of wealth creation, but it's often misunderstood. We all strive to increase our income, believing that it's the key to a better life. However, the truth is that it's not just about how much money you make; it's also about how much you keep and what you do with the money you keep that truly matters.

I invite you—no, I *implore* you—to shift your focus from solely increasing your income to mastering the art of retaining and growing your wealth. It's a subtle yet powerful shift that will allow you to take control of your financial destiny and open doors to a life you never thought possible. That said, though, we will explore ways to increase your income in Part III.

Driver #2: Savings Rate

The second Wealth Driver, the *savings rate*, is the lifeblood of your financial success. It's the percentage of your income that you're putting away for your future. No matter your current financial situation, I urge you to push your savings rate as high as you possibly can. We actually tell our clients that as part of the Wealth Priority Ladder, we want them in the 20 to 30 percent range depending on their age or stage of life.

Many people say they can't put money away, but if you can save even five dollars, then start there. Remember, it's more about the behaviors than the amount. Embrace the behavior change, for it's akin to building a muscle. When you first go to the gym, you don't begin by lifting the heaviest weights. You start small and gradually increase your strength. There's no shame in starting with just five dollars; the key is to begin exercising the wealth-creation muscle. It will grow over time, and before you know it, your small savings will have transformed into a substantial fortune.

In general, people do not make saving or investing a priority. The Wealth Priority Pathway™ shows the difference between those that struggle financially and those that have better control of their money. Most people make money, spend money to fund their lifestyle, and then look at what's left to use for investing. But if you're real with yourself, you'll see that this method literally builds your financial future on the scraps that are left over. Those that build wealth consistently flip this to put investing as the priority over spending.

I can hear you now: "Mel, I can't; I'm barely making ends meet now!" I get it. But part of your journey in this book will be to know specifically where every dollar is going and what it's for, then looking for ways to maximize your income while managing the spending.

THE WEALTH PRIORITY PATHWAY ™

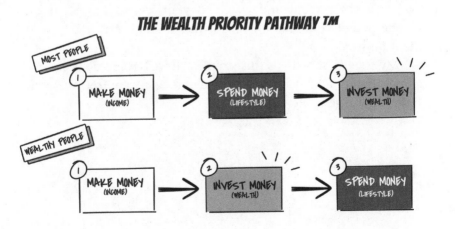

Driver #3: Investment Returns

The third Wealth Driver, *investment returns*, represents the life-changing power of compounding. It's about how much you're making on your investments—and the key here is to strike a delicate balance between risk and reward.

As you strive for higher returns, understand that there's a trade-off between the potential gains and the risks involved. It's why a certificate of deposit (CD) often pays you less than 1 percent, while riskier investments offer higher returns—they're compensating you for the risks you're taking. Embrace the challenge, for mastering this balance can be the catalyst that propels you toward financial freedom. We'll talk more in depth about this in Part III.

Driver #4: Time

Of the four Wealth Drivers, *time* is the most important and also the most elusive. We don't control time except for one crucial aspect: this very moment. The present is where your power lies, and it's up to you to seize it. The answer to the time question in the Wealth Drivers Matrix is today—or now—because we can't control it otherwise.

Every day that goes by is an opportunity to invest in your future, and to make choices that will bring you closer to the life you desire. Don't let time slip through your fingers. Harness the power of the present and watch as your wealth grows, fueled by the potent combination of income, savings rate, and investment returns.

My friends, it really is this simple. All we have to do is change simple habits and decisions in order to gain control over our finances and generate wealth.

CHAPTER 3

CONQUERING YOUR FINANCIAL FEARS

When we are no longer able to change a situation . . .
we are challenged to change ourselves.

— VIKTOR FRANKL

Beyond the main excuses, there's one other demon that can get in your way, and it's the "F" word. Yep, *fear.*

Have you ever found yourself on the brink of a financial decision, only to freeze, unable to move forward? Many people experience this paralysis, and after digging deeper, we often discover that fear lies at the heart of the struggle.

The truth is, people aren't afraid of making decisions; they're afraid of making the *wrong* decisions. But here's the challenge: fear prevents us from fully committing, from being present in the moment, and from giving our all. When we show up with half of what we could give and we don't get the results that we want, we start to validate ourselves and say, "See? I shouldn't have done it." But did we really try? Did we really give it everything we had? To achieve extraordinary results, we must be willing to pay the price—not in dollars, but in effort, lessons, and determination. You can't achieve greatness without putting in the work.

Courageousness is what we need, and courageousness is a choice. Have the courage to do things that are uncomfortable, the courage to be willing to commit, and the courage to step up. So instead of, "How do I make a million dollars?" ask instead, "Do I have the courage to step in and do the things that make millionaires?" It won't actually be a reality if you're not willing to do the work you need to do.

Do you have the courage to make the decisions you need to and get the results that you want?

Wealth is a mere number—a statistic, a figure in a bank account. What we truly seek is the richness of life that wealth can provide.

What I've found is that fear is really an indication that something is lacking when it comes to your ability to make a decision. Let's deal with fear head-on, because once we eliminate the excuses and the fear, nothing will hold us back from creating a Money Machine.

THE LACK STACK OF FEAR™

To help you conquer your financial fears, I offer a six-part framework that replaces fear with understanding, confidence, and courage. It's called the Lack Stack of Fear.

1. Lack of Clarity

Lack of clarity can cause fear simply because it causes uncertainty in direction, purpose, and process. First, identify what you want and why you want it. Clarity concerning your destination and purpose can help dispel uncertainty and empower you to make decisions. Recognize the source of your fears and confront past mistakes to gain a clearer understanding of how to move forward.

2. Lack of Information

When we don't have enough good information to make a clear decision, it shows up as fear in our financial decisions. Arm yourself with the necessary knowledge before investing in something. Lack of information can stall decision-making, so ensure you gather all the facts and consider risk-reversal options, such as refund policies or guarantees.

THE LACK STACK OF FEAR ™

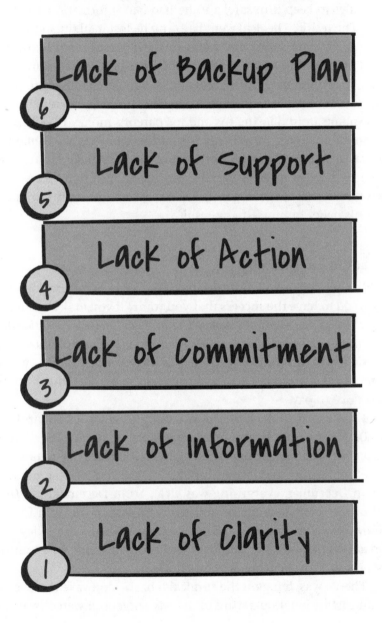

One of my clients, Mark, put a lot of money into a real estate deal back in the mid-2000s. He even used a bunch of his parents' money. He didn't have a process or system to follow. He didn't have any rules to keep him safe, and he had bad information given to him. The result? The deal went bad, and he lost it all (including his parents' money). From that point forward, he assumed he wasn't good at investing and just put money in a savings account that didn't pay out much return, figuring he was going to have to work the rest of his life instead of building wealth. He had so much guilt and shame around losing his and his parents' money that he took on an identity that wasn't true. Using the Money Story Dynamic, he was able to separate the stories from the facts and get clarity on what he needed to do, where he was going, and how to use this newfound knowledge to get there. He turned around his finances and his belief in himself as a result.

3. Lack of Commitment

This might be hard to confront, but let's face it: What are you willing to do to have the success that you want? If you look at your life and think, *I don't have the money I want; I don't have the relationship I want; I don't have the body or the health that I want*, you must also consider whether you've paid the price to earn them. Now, we all deserve everything in life; that's my firm belief. But there might be a price to pay.

I got a real understanding of commitment back in April of 2020. After I was diagnosed with cancer in June 2019, I went through two surgeries: one in July, one in August. They removed a couple of tumors, and I went through 36 treatments in six months, but in December, everything was clear. So in December of 2019, I thought this whole cancer journey was behind me, and I went on my way. On April 24, 2020, I had just finished a three-day live virtual event, and I went in for what I thought would be a routine scope and scan, figuring all was still clear.

There I was, lying on the surgical table, wide awake in the cold of an institutional operating room. My surgeon towered over me with his full six-foot-four-inch frame, doing the scope. I stared at him intently, trying to catch a tell or sign of what he saw, if anything. But he had this stoic poker face until I heard him say, "Oh, that's something." My eyes got wide, and I felt all the air leave my lungs when I realized he had found another tumor—the cancer was back. So, here I was, thinking I was clear, and then four months later they found another tumor, which put me in a spiral again.

Four days later, a good friend of mine asked how I was holding up, and I admitted I wasn't good. "How clear are you on the outcome?" he asked.

"On the outcome, or the *desired* outcome?" I returned.

He said they should be one and the same. The truth of that hit hard.

I said to him, "I will beat this again."

Then he asked the question that sent me into such an extreme level of commitment and conviction that the cancer never stood a chance. "Well, if you knew the outcome today, what would you do each day to make that the reality you live into?"

That conversation made me realize that even though I don't know how each day is going to unfold, I do know what the destination is, and I'm committed to reaching it. I had to clarify the destination. I also had more information because we started to look at other treatment protocols to achieve it, so it increased my level of clarity and decreased my level of fear. Then I increased my commitment to do what it takes, one day at a time.

The fact of the matter is, if we're only *interested* in building wealth, but we're not *committed*, we won't change our behaviors. To change our habits, we will be forced to change our decisions. These habits and decisions change our behaviors, which finally changes our results in all aspects of our life. I hope this is landing for you.

When your *why* is big enough, it will drive the commitment. Get a grasp of the why that drives your soul—not intellectually, but to the core of your being—and you'll see that you can move mountains.

When I got diagnosed with cancer, I was eating healthy, working out six days a week, wasn't a smoker, barely drank, and was doing everything I was "supposed" to do. A doctor revealed to me, "Mel, sugar fuels cancer. I know you have a sweet tooth, so what can you do to stop or at least reduce it?" In that moment, I looked at my life and thought about how much I love my wife, my son, his wife, their kids, and my life. If sugar was fueling cancer and cancer is death, then sugar was now equated to death. Quitting sugar became an easy choice to commit to.

I literally went on a three-day water fast to break my connection to sugar, and I haven't looked back. I am sure that my diet still has some sugars, but I'm diligent in avoiding anything with processed sugar or added sugar. My reason to live is stronger than my habit of having a sweet tooth. My why was strong enough to get me to commit to what was necessary.

Your financial future should be meaningful for you. This isn't about money in a bank account; this is about your children and your grandchildren. It's about the causes, the missions, the movements you want to get behind, and the change you want to see in the world that you get a chance to fund. This is about being able to buy back the moments of your life in a way that you get to live it by choice, to have a life of "I get to" instead of "I have to." To be able to do that, you're required to have the ability to say no to things that don't suit you today.

I'm urging you to look at where you are and say, "I am committed to a new financial future. I am committed to a new financial trajectory, not just for me but for my family."

What is your *why*? Ask yourself what you're willing to do to achieve your financial goals. When your why is big enough, it will drive the commitment needed to change your habits, decisions, and behaviors, ultimately transforming your life.

4. Lack of Action

Even if you clear up the first three levels of fear, if you don't take action, your fear will overcome you. Actions will give rise to understanding and clarity so you can continue with better information to move forward.

Your actions reveal your true priorities and values. Take small, consistent steps over time to make a significant impact. Sometimes it's starting with a small decision first. Let's just move money into a high-yield cash account automatically. Let's start with $50 per week. Can we do that? It's a small decision, a small commitment, but a big step. It's the same reason we use dollar-cost averaging—which is taking small, consistent steps over time—to invest into the market. Over 30 years, $50 per week turns into $300,000. If you can put away $1,500 per month, it turns into $2.2 million. Small actions done consistently over time make a huge difference. Begin with what's available to you and gradually build upon your progress.

5. Lack of Support

When we feel isolated or siloed, we tend to freeze with the fear of making a bad or wrong decision. But having the right people around you can make it easier to walk the path you're meant to walk, no matter how uncertain it may be. Surround yourself with a team that understands your financial vision and can help you achieve it. Money, investing, and wealth have always been such taboo topics in our country, which leaves so many people ill-equipped to handle money or at risk of making poor money decisions. Have more conversations around these topics with the people who matter to you. Include your spouse or maybe a coach, mentor, or advisor. Get them to understand your vision and to hold you to the standard required to make the vision a reality. The truth of the matter is, things may pop up throughout your journey that block your way.

Back in 2004, I made one of the worst money and investing decisions of my life. I got involved in an investment that I thought was going to be amazing, but it ended up costing me one-third of everything I owned. It was devastating, to say the least. Between me and my two friends who got involved, we lost over $4.5 million in what turned out to be a Ponzi scheme and not an investment. Needless to say, I beat myself up something awful, especially being a CPA and financial guy that people come to for guidance.

How could I be so stupid? What did I miss? I started to question whether I should consider a profession change. But had I taken that path, Stefanie and I would never have been in the financial position we're in today, and I certainly would not be writing this book.

Fortunately, I have people in my corner who saw me spiraling and did what amounted to an intervention of sorts. They got me to reflect on and appreciate my skills, my capabilities, and my responsibilities (my main one being Jeremy at the time).

Those around me whom I respected and who supported me said, "The lesson Jeremy takes from this will be with him the rest of his life, and it depends on how you respond in this moment. Do you want him to see you curled up in the corner giving up or see you taking the skills you know you have that built everything in the first place and come through it triumphantly?"

The answer was clear. Truth be told, the same things I'm teaching you here actually allowed me to get back on my feet and not only recover what was lost but to surpass it by three times from where I had started within 18 months.

This is the power of a support group. You need someone you can talk with about alternatives, someone who supports you to pivot when needed but never to give up—because you're

ACTION ITEM

Make a list of the people who matter to you. Do they understand your vision? Will they act as your support group and hold you to the standard required to make the vision a reality? Commit to having more money conversations with them today.

committed. These folks can be your safety net when you falter, your sanity when you feel crazed, and your cheerleaders who celebrate you. Wealth creation, financial freedom, and living a rich life were never meant to be solo pursuits.

6. Lack of a Backup Plan

When we only have one way of achieving results, it raises the stakes, escalates the stress, and causes you the angst of knowing you have a single point of failure. Develop a contingency plan to address any obstacles or setbacks that may arise on your financial journey. But do it and test it before you start so you have the options at your fingertips if things go the wrong way. This is one of the reasons we continually stress-test a financial plan once we create it. We must see how sound the plan is and what the impact is when things go wrong—even when they go right. It's like a seat belt in a car: better to have it on and not need it than not to have it on and realize you need it.

* * *

And that's how we step through fear. I use this framework myself when I feel the pull of fear, and I do the same with my clients when they're going through financial decisions that seem to be weighing on them.

Do we have clarity? Do we have all the information we need to make the decision? Are we committed? Are we taking action? Do we have a support team? Do we have a backup plan? If we walk through this journey with confidence and courage, our success skyrockets and fear shrinks. This is your checklist. Use it to keep you on your path to financial freedom. When you do, you'll be more equipped, more committed, more informed, and more resolute if things go awry, because you have the steps to correct it.

CHAPTER 4

AFFLUENCE ISN'T OPULENCE—IT'S MUCH MORE!

Richness in life is measured in the things that money can't buy.

— MEL ABRAHAM

My cancer diagnosis made me realize that everyone needs a Money Machine to live a life of richness, one that they measure not just by money but also value, depth, and meaning. Folks who hear me speak about the idea of living an affluent life often confuse *affluence* with *opulence*, and that isn't what I mean.

A rich, affluent life is about the quality of the moments we create, and money is only a tool that allows us to control those special moments. There are four aspects of the Affluent Life Paradigm™, and only one of them has anything to do with money.

Living an affluent life is meaningful (we have joy from the inside), impactful (we have a positive impact on those we serve and love), fruitful (we build wealth), and peaceful (we're walking on a path that's aligned with our values and vision).

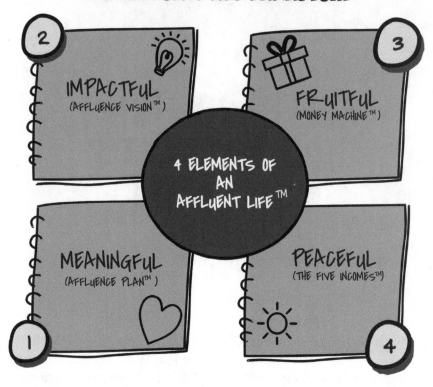

CREATE AN AFFLUENCE PLAN, NOT A FINANCIAL PLAN

Reaching financial freedom is not just about creating a financial plan; it's about understanding what you want your life to be, what you want it to look like, and what you want it to feel like. It's about planning for the lifestyle you want to live and the process to get there, which is what I call the Affluence Plan™.

This is likely a different approach to your finances than any you've ever taken before, even if you've worked closely with a team of financial experts. The truth is, the financial services industry isn't always working in your best interest (which I'll discuss further in Part III). I wrote this book to give you access to trusted, unbiased financial advice that puts your dreams and goals at the forefront. I don't have financial investments to sell, so I'm able to help you make choices that benefit you without bias based on commissions or quotas. I am focused on putting you back in the captain's chair so that you are in control of your financial destiny.

Here's the thing: I don't know where you are in your life. I don't know what struggles you might be dealing with. I don't know what your journey has been financially or otherwise. Like I said earlier, I believe financial freedom to be your birthright. Now, I get it; it may not always be easy depending on where you're at currently, but it's certainly simple when you understand the principles, the processes, and the priorities you need in order to make it happen. The only thing you need to add is the desire, dedication, and discipline to apply them to your life so they become your reality.

In a 2018 study of 4,000 millionaires, researchers at Harvard Business School found that one of the key drivers of happiness was *how* the millionaires generated their wealth instead of the amount of wealth itself.[1] This is important to note: *How* they created their wealth mattered to their happiness because of the meaningfulness it gave them in the process, not just the outcome. They did something that mattered; they did something that gave them the opportunity to live a wealthy life.

Studies show that an affluent life is empty without meaningfulness and impact driving it. Instead, true wealth is about having a *richer* life, a deeper impact, and more freedom. I need to be able to make money to pay the bills, but that alone doesn't create affluence, and that's the mistake a lot of people make when thinking about living an affluent life. Paying the bills doesn't drive affluence; having a meaningful purpose does.

To have a meaningful life, you need an Affluence Plan. This isn't a *financial* plan per se, but a plan that looks at and examines your life. It's about understanding what you want your life to be, what you want it to look like, and what you want it to feel like in order to move toward those things intentionally. While it's true that your goals may be achieved even without a plan, if it was done haphazardly or by coincidence, we can't guarantee the results can be replicated over time.

You want to have a specific plan in place for the lifestyle you want to live and also the process to make the plan your reality. This is much bigger and more detailed than a vision board. An Affluence Plan is a true plan with steps to execute and milestones to reach.

By now I hope you see the need to take back control of your financial destiny and that you actually have the ability to do it no matter your age or stage. You see the possibility of what your life could be like to live affluently and how it will change generations beyond you when done right. It's no longer about lots of money but the right behaviors done over time, and not allowing the excuses, stories, or fear overtake you and your birthright of financial freedom.

So, what are the steps? What's the process? What's the path?

Creating your Affluence Plan is the framework of Part II. Simply put, we're going to understand where you are now, define where you want to go, and give you the process to close the gap between the two.

Your Future (Chapters 5 and 6) is about creating a vivid and emotionally compelling vision on all levels of your life.

Your Reality (Chapters 7 and 8) is about getting really honest with your income, expenses, and spending and saving habits.

Your Gap (Chapters 9 and 10) is the space in the middle that your wealth-building journey will fill. Too often, we spend an inordinate amount of time either dreaming about the destination or lamenting our reality. Both are laden with inaction. But when you use them instead as guideposts for action, things change— and they can change quickly.

There will be moments in the next several chapters where my tone will change, and I will be very direct. Know that it's coming from a place of compassion because I know what this plan can do for your life, and I hope you take it in the spirit in which it's intended. I want you to have a Money Machine so you can reach financial freedom, so you can live life exactly how you dream of experiencing it—in the most meaningful and value-aligned way possible. I want the absolute best for you, and I know that this Money Machine can help you attain it.

Ready? Let's go.

Part II

DEFINE THE JOURNEY

Investing isn't for the wealthy;
it is the path to wealthy.

— MEL ABRAHAM

Your Future

Dreaming isn't enough.
You need to turn the dream into a plan.

— MEL ABRAHAM

CHAPTER 5

GAINING FINANCIAL CONTROL WITH CLARITY

The only limit to our realization of
tomorrow will be our doubts of today.

— FRANKLIN D. ROOSEVELT

On July 4, 1952, Florence Chadwick, a renowned long-distance swimmer, set out to become the first woman to swim across the roughly 21-mile Catalina Channel off the California coast. Despite having previously swum the English Channel, Florence found this attempt challenging due to heavy fog and cold, shark-infested waters. After swimming for 16 exhausting hours, she looked up at her rescue boat and admitted defeat. She couldn't go any farther. When they pulled her into the boat, they revealed the heartbreaking truth—she was less than a mile from the shore.

Florence returned 60 days later with a clear vision of her destination, a newfound commitment, and a solid plan in place. This time, she completed the swim in just 14 hours. The difference? She was more committed to her outcome, and she had a clearer vision throughout the process. She could see where she was going, and she kept it in view the whole time without fog overtaking it.

The power to change where you go is within you. Like Florence Chadwick, you simply need to have a vivid vision that you keep in view.

THE BROKEN RETIREMENT PARADIGM: WHY YOU NEED AN AFFLUENCE VISION

It's amazing how many people live their lives without a clear vision of where they want to be in the future. They become trapped in societal expectations and limited by their own self-imposed boundaries. The result is a life filled with uncertainty, financial stress, and unfulfilled dreams.

It's time to break free from this cycle and chart a course for the life you truly desire. To do so, you must first answer a crucial question: *Where do you want to go?*

Creating a detailed vision of your future is essential to making informed decisions and crafting a plan to achieve your goals. As you work toward your objectives in your Affluence Plan, you must remain mindful of the time-sensitive nature of financial planning. Time is an invaluable asset, and the sooner you act, the better prepared you will be now, as well as for your golden years.

Unfortunately, many people reach retirement age and end up facing financial hardships and limited options because they never had a vivid vision. Here are some shocking stats that will blow you away:[1]

AGE RANGE	MEDIAN RETIREMENT SAVINGS
under age 25	about $1,800
Ages 25–34	about $14,100
Ages 35–44	$36,100+
Ages 45–54	$61,500+
Ages 55–64	$89,700+
Ages 65+	$87,700+

SOURCE: Vanguard "How America Saves 2022" Data

This is especially worrisome when you consider that the average medical cost for a retired couple during their retirement years will accumulate to $315,000.[2] And that's for just the *expected* medical costs.

If you think the traditional retirement plan you have set up is enough, I want to be clear that it is *not enough*. I hate to break it to you, but the traditional retirement system is not working, and many people are finding themselves without enough savings to retire, let alone maintain the lifestyle they envision after retirement.

As an industrial-age country, the United States had a retirement system that was originally built on the idea that after working for a company for most of one's life, that person would receive a pension in exchange for their loyalty. A pension meant receiving lifetime income based on one's earnings. However, with people living longer and the rising of costs, traditional pension plans became too expensive for most companies to sustain, and they've generally moved away from that model.

To replace the pension, the government introduced IRAs and 401(k)s in 1974 and 1978, respectively. However, there's a problem with this newer model. These accounts will not replace the pension if it's not run properly, because the government limits the amount that you can put into it, and it doesn't produce lifetime income. People are unaware of this problem until it's too late.

The broken retirement model suggests that once you retire, you're supposed to live out the rest of your days on a reduced lifestyle. Often this means dropping your spending to 70 percent of what you're used to. As a result, many retirees end up spending their retirement savings to maintain their lifestyle, which can quickly drain their funds. The save, reduce, spend, and pray mentality is literally a race to the end in hopes that your life doesn't outlast your money.

THE BROKEN RETIREMENT PARADIGM

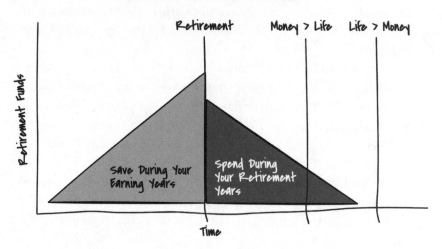

After dedicating your life to work for all those years, why should you have to reduce your lifestyle? You should be able to maintain it or, even better, elevate it.

But one thing is for certain: the broken retirement system and the shift of the responsibility for creating your lifetime income onto you instead of the company you work for is why it's so important to create a Money Machine today. A well-defined Affluence Plan allows you to identify where you are, where you're going, and the steps necessary to close the gap between the two. It looks a bit like this:

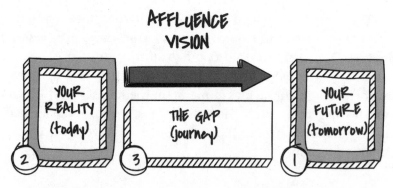

Your Affluence Vision is built from your future lifestyle backward.

It's natural to feel apprehensive about the journey ahead, but knowledge is power. By understanding your current situation and the distance to your goals, you can take the necessary steps to bridge the gap, reclaim your financial power, and embark on the path to success. So let's start by defining your future.

CHAPTER 6

DEFINE YOUR FUTURE FIRST

Let the dreams inform the path.

— MEL ABRAHAM

To chart your path toward financial freedom, let's begin by clar-ifying your vision. Crafting your Affluence Vision can be a chal-lenging, reflective process, but it's the heavy lifting that sets the foundation for your future.

Too often, retirement calculators and financial tools fail to count these things as a crucial step, but understanding your desires and the reasons behind them will fuel your drive and discipline to make them a reality. Plus, you then have a clear idea of what your finish line looks like. This is why when I work with clients, we build their financial structure from the lifestyle in, not the income out. Here's what I mean by this: Many advisors and planners will look at your current income level and use that as the baseline for planning your golden years. But using your income as the starting point doesn't consider what you truly want as the ultimate destination. Remember, your money deci-sions today should be in service of the future you want to create tomorrow. So let's start with that and reverse engineer the path to get you there.

STEP 1: CRAFT YOUR VISION, LAYER BY LAYER

Instead of asking the overwhelming question, "What's your vision for your life?" we'll break it down into manageable layers I call *domains*. You'll spend time journaling about what you want your life to look like in each of the following domains:

1. Family and Relationships
2. Career and Business
3. Health and Wellness
4. Financial Security
5. Lifestyle
6. Contribution and Legacy

DOMAINS OF LIFE

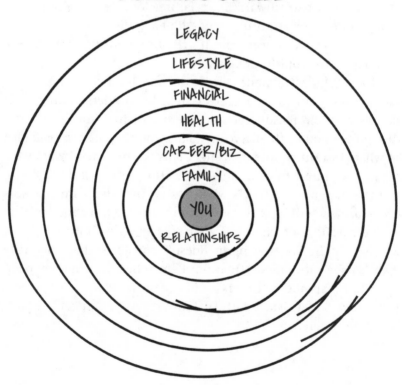

For each domain, we'll explore three core questions:

1. What is your ideal scenario within each domain?

2. What does each domain mean to you?

3. What words come to mind when you think about each of these domains?

We'll do this step-by-step. Be sure to take your time with each of these, and answer them wholly and completely to get the most out of the journey ahead.

Domain #1: Family and Relationships

Consider the relationships that matter most to you—family, friends, and professional connections. Break them into subsections if necessary.

- What does the perfect scenario for each relationship look like to you?

- How would you describe the importance of each type of relationship in your life?

- Which terms or phrases best capture the essence of these meaningful relationships?

Domain #2: Career and Business

Picture your dream career or business venture, considering income, status, environment, and advancement.

- What does your ideal career look like and what makes it so appealing to you?

- Can you explain the personal significance behind your ideal professional life?

- What words or phrases come to mind when you consider your ultimate career or business aspirations?

Domain #3: Health and Wellness

Envision your ideal state of health, and contemplate its importance in your life, considering such specific details as your weight, body composition, energy, feelings, and vibrancy.

- What does ideal health look like for you?

- Why is achieving this level of health essential in your life?

- Which words or ideas come to mind when you contemplate your optimal health?

Domain #4: Financial Security

Define your ideal financial state, considering income and assets.

- What does financial security mean to you? What does it look like?

- How does financial security factor into your life's higher purpose?

- What terms or ideas resonate with you when you think about achieving financial well-being?

Domain #5: Lifestyle

Imagine your perfect lifestyle in the years to come.

- What elements of your ideal lifestyle are most special to you?

- Why is it important for you to live this specific way of life?

- What words embody your desired way of living?

Domain #6: Contribution and Legacy

Dream about the great contribution and legacy you hope to leave behind.

- What does your ideal legacy look like to you?

- What is the personal significance behind your envisioned contribution and legacy?

- What words or phrases best describe the positive difference you hope to make in the world?

Pull out your journal and start writing! Get specific and clear on each of these questions. Within each domain, dream big and make your vision meaningful. If there are additional domains of importance in your life (such as religion or spirituality), you can add those and use the same three core questions to guide you.

This is an invitation to explore the depths of your desires and aspirations to understand what success and affluence mean to you.

Embrace this process to craft a life that is authentically yours. Connect your aspirations to your heart and soul, ensuring they resonate deeply within you. Remember, this is about creating a life that is uniquely yours, based on your values, desires, and aspirations. It's about making it so emotionally compelling that it energizes and excites you when you think about living at that level.

As an example, here are mine from a number of years ago for financial security and relationships.

FINANCIAL

QUESTIONS

Completely financially liberated. minimum of $10million in investable assets, leveraged income potential at >80%, no debt, trusts and wealth plans in place

This will change my life and my whole family tree's lives. It will give me the peace of mind of knowing all is good and my wife and family are all taken care of. I get to make in an impact and create a leveraged legacy...richness of life

liberated, richness, wealth, liquid, debt free, peace of mind, experience without guilt or stress, informed

WORDS

RELATIONSHIPS

QUESTIONS

A relationship that is full of experiences, joy, love and friendship. A partner in life with a shared vision.

Friends that are loyal but challenge me...that are independent yet there for me...value our word and the bond between us.

Sharing life with others is what give my life more richness and joy. Being able to better others through my relationship allows me to live some of my highest ideals.

Loving, richness, experiences, trust, dependability, travel, joy, fun, laughter, empathy, caring

WORDS

STEP 2: KNOW WHAT YOU WANT, DON'T WANT

After exploring these domains, move on to what I call the Want, Don't Want exercise. This liberating brain dump will help clarify your desires and aversions, making it easier to understand the actions you're willing to take—or avoid—on your journey. It will also provide a clearer understanding of your priorities and boundaries.

Make two columns on a sheet of paper, and label one side "Want" and the other "Don't Want." Brain dump all the words or short statements representing what you want and don't want in your life. Get real with yourself. The more real you are, the more powerful you will find this process.

These are mine from my journal:

WANT	DON'T WANT
health, vibrancy, love, friends, financial security, deep relationships, meaningful interactions, family, compelling future, living my values, ideals, profitable business, doing what I love, travel, fun experiences, laughter, joy, walking with my wife	cancer, friction, stress, decline, anger, doing things that have no meaning, living to work, negativity, pettiness, repeat mistakes of the past, losing sight of my vision and purpose, being alone, not being appreciated

The Want, Don't Want exercise helps set boundaries for the lifestyle you want. Your lifestyle will be a result of your values, how you show up, the work you're willing to put in, and the decisions you make around your money.

STEP 3: UNDERSTAND YOUR MONEY'S PURPOSE

As you start to move toward your financial freedom, you will hit obstacles. And when you hit them, it's the money's purpose that moves you through. Money's purpose goes beyond its basic function as a medium of exchange for goods and services. It represents the means to achieve your various goals and fulfill personal values in your life, helping you step into your own purpose. The fact is, when you give your money a higher purpose, you rise to a higher purpose. (Read that again.)

This phenomenon showed up in a conversation I had with one of my clients:

"Mel, you're probably the only one I could have this conversation with that would understand," Alison said.

"What's up?" I asked.

"I hit all my numbers already this year!" she replied.

I sensed that she was happy, but not with the ecstatic happiness that you would expect from someone that just hit their numbers—and trust me, the numbers were big.

I probed more. "Why is it I get you're not excited about this?"

She confided that she actually was happy, but she was confused because she wasn't sure what to do next. She asked me, "What do I do? Just keep increasing the numbers? But it then starts to feel like I'm just chasing an arbitrary number and always going for more just for the sake of having more."

This is why you need to know your *why* before *how* or *how much*. The fact is that money is a *result* and not a *purpose*. It's also the reason we start the process of building the Money Machine with creating an Affluence Vision. Without attaching your financial vision to a proper *why* and a higher purpose, the difficult times can become even more difficult. But more important, even "successful" times can feel empty without a purpose.

Alison's passion and purpose was giving women in developing countries the opportunity for financial independence. In the end, we restructured her business so that with every sale she made, she would sponsor a microloan to a needy woman. Now here's the beautiful thing: she would do it in the name of the customer who purchased it and not her own.

Shortly after we did this, I got this text from her after she finished a big promotional launch.

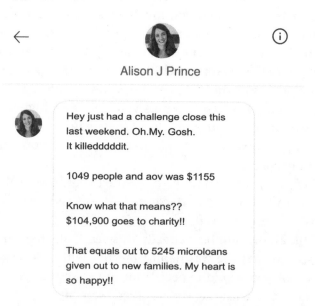

←   Alison J Prince   ⓘ

Hey just had a challenge close this last weekend. Oh.My. Gosh. It killedddddit.

1049 people and aov was $1155

Know what that means?? $104,900 goes to charity!!

That equals out to 5245 microloans given out to new families. My heart is so happy!!

Since that day, she has sponsored thousands more microloans.

The point is that accumulating wealth for no purpose other than to stockpile assets is an empty pursuit. It doesn't have the same force of energy as an inspired vision to break through barriers or get through challenging times.

Have you ever paused to consider the true purpose behind your pursuit of money? Are you simply chasing after dollars without understanding why you desire them? More to the point, are you accumulating wealth without achieving true richness in your life? Let's take a moment to explore the concept of purpose, its role in our lives, and how understanding the purpose of money can lead to a more fulfilling existence.

The pursuit of purpose can be a daunting task, often accompanied by feelings of uncertainty and anxiety. We want a purpose that we feel is authentic; however, it's important to understand that purpose does not guarantee happiness. You must also recognize that you may have multiple purposes throughout your life, serving different roles and people. My purposes as a spouse, father, grandfather, and mentor are all different. Sometimes, a purpose is only meant for a season, allowing us to fully embrace the present moment.

Purpose may also be shared with others, like in the case of a married couple who bring their individual and combined purposes to the relationship. It's crucial to remember that your purpose can be revealed and evolve over time. As you journey through life, embracing the process of discovery can be a beautiful experience. If you're unsure of your purpose, consider these three keys to unveiling it:

1. Be open to the possibility that your purpose may lie on a different path than the one you're currently on or that it may already be the path you've chosen. Accept that this journey may not always be joyous, but it serves a purpose that may not yet be apparent.

2. Cultivate the courage to act. Recognize when you're unhappy and make a change. My twin brother

worked for someone for 35 years and hated and dreaded it every day. It wasn't until he finally admitted that he wasn't destined for that and found the openness to accept it that he then had the courage to act and change his situation.

3. Dedicate yourself to becoming who you were meant to be. Live your life fully expressed, immersed, and experienced so that when you reach the end of your days, you can look back with peace in your heart.

As you explore your purpose, be mindful of any self-imposed barriers or stories that might hold you back. (You may want to refer back to the information on money stories, excuses, and fears in Chapters 2 and 3.) When we acknowledge and overcome these obstacles, we become open to accepting our purpose, developing the courage to act, and dedicating ourselves to growth.

In Paulo Coelho's *The Alchemist,* the protagonist, Santiago, discovers that his purpose is right in front of him, but a lack of openness prevents him from seeing it. For me, it took a cancer diagnosis and a global pandemic to recognize my purpose as a financial mentor.

Purpose is not a destination, but a journey. Purpose is something that just unfolds. As you start to understand money, you will realize money is not a purpose. That's why people chasing dollars always feel unfulfilled and unhappy in the end. There is a difference between richness in life versus wealth in life. Richness is experiences and feelings. Money is a fuel, it's a tool, it's energy.

When I give my money greater purpose, my money gives *me* greater purpose. So it's not about the purchasing power of the money that matters but the delivery of the enrichment in life that it creates. So, do you know the purpose of your money?

Creating a money purpose statement is an effective way to guide our financial decisions and behaviors. This statement acts as a filter for our choices, encouraging us to become more purposeful with our wealth. Without money purpose statements, it's easy to fall into the trap of old money stories. Let's take someone who didn't have money growing up. Maybe they lived paycheck to paycheck, their parents lived paycheck to paycheck, and they were in debt; maybe there were foreclosures and bad experiences in their life. All of a sudden, they have money but they're out there spending wildly and just can't figure out why they have no wealth.

Well, what happens if the spender has this money purpose statement instead: *My money's purpose in my life is to provide security and peace of mind to my family and me while allowing me to live my truest joy?* Every time the spender makes a financial decision, they run it through this filter. They ask themselves: *Will my choice provide security and peace of mind to my family and me, plus allow me to live my truest joy?* If the answer is no, all of a sudden the spender doesn't become a spender; they become someone that is purposeful with their wealth.

My money's purpose in my life is to help me connect and create while serving people, missions, and causes I align with. So I run the financial decisions I make through that filter. Our money purpose statement starts to drive the choices and the decisions we make because the fact of the matter is, wealth creation is a behavior. It's not about money statistics; it's not even about how much we earn. It's a behavior, and if we shift our behaviors, our money changes.

ACTION ITEM

Now it's your turn. Take a moment to craft your money purpose statement. First, consider how you want to show up for your money and how your money will serve you in return. Then, beginning with the phrase, "Money's purpose in my life is _____," fill in the blank with what you want your money to do for you.

Ensure that your money purpose statement resonates with you emotionally, allowing you to feel a powerful connection when you say it aloud. Draft your statement. Print it. Envision the positive changes it will bring to your life, and display it somewhere visible as a daily reminder of your journey ahead.

As we continue to explore the intertwining relationship between money and purpose, it's essential to keep in mind that our ultimate goal is not simply to accumulate wealth but to achieve true richness in our lives. By understanding the purpose of your money, you can use it as a powerful tool for personal growth and fulfillment, ultimately creating a life that is not only wealthy but truly rich in meaning, experiences, and connections.

STEP 4: CREATE A CONTRACT WITH YOUR FUTURE SELF

Now that you have a clear vision of what you want in each of the important layers of your life, let's focus specifically on the next 10 years in order to set tangible goals.

Take a moment to imagine your life specifically in 10 years from now. How old will you be? What do you see? How do you feel? To truly be clear on and create the life you desire, it's essential to craft a personalized vision statement that acts as a contract with yourself, defining the life you want and holding you accountable for making it a reality.

Begin by considering the following statements (but don't start writing yet):

- In 10 years, I am _____ years old.

- In 10 years, I feel _____.

- In 10 years, I am _____.

- In 10 years, I contribute by _____
  _____.

- In 10 years, my achievements include _____
  _____.

- In 10 years, I've experienced _____
  _____.

- In 10 years, I love _____.

- In 10 years, I'm surrounded by _____.

- In 10 years, I'm a point of inspiration and influence for _____.
- In 10 years, I'm helping to bring into the world ____ _____.

Here's an example of what my answers looked like a few years ago:

SETTING YOUR VISION & GOALS

In 10 years, I am __68__ years old.

In 10 years, I feel __Satisfied, happy, vibrant, loving & significant__.

In 10 years, I am __traveling with my wife, sharing life, serving & being a messenger of possibility__.

In 10 years, I contribute by __speaking, serving, teaching & mentoring, also financially free__

In 10 years, my achievements include __loving husband/father, 1,000's financially free__.

In 10 years, I've experienced __fun, joy, pain, growth, living, traveling, loving, freedom__

In 10 years, I love __my wife, my life & those that are in my life. Sharing & serving__.

In 10 years, I'm surrounded by __family & friends that matter. Colleagues that challenge & support me.__

In 10 years, I'm a point of inspiration and influence for __my son/grandkids & those I serve__

In 10 years, I'm helping to bring into the world __Financial liberation, freedom & possibility of living your dreams again__

ACTION ITEM

Now it's your turn. Answer the 10 vision and goal questions for yourself in your journal. The more specific you are, the more powerful your answers will be. Write in the present tense, as if it has all come to pass already.

With this clear vision in your mind, you can now create a contract, a promise to your future self. Take another page in your journal and write a heartfelt, detailed description of your ideal life in 10 years. Describe it as if it's already happening, using the present tense and positive language. For example, "I am 100 percent debt-free, 100 percent cancer-free, and celebrating my 20th wedding anniversary with my beautiful wife." This is your letter of commitment to yourself and to the future you envision.

Focus on what you want, not what you don't want, as the subconscious mind can't distinguish between positive and negative thoughts.

Here's my letter of commitment from a few years back:

SETTING YOUR VISION & GOALS

In 10 years, I will be 100% debt free, 100% cancer free and going on my 20th year of marriage to my beautiful bride Stefanie. We will have our place by the beach but also be spending long sabbaticals in exotic places around the world to experience new things and share in new cultures. We will likely be grandparents.

I will have a lucrative online business around helping people become financially liberated through entrepreneurship. I will have written at least 2 more books and be speaking at conferences while being a highly sought after commentator on business and financial matters.

I will be running my high level masterminds to work with my hand-picked clients to build their life by design and financial plan to liberation.

I feel grateful, satisfied, happy and joyous. I appreciate life and what life has given me. I get to contribute through my work and serve those that are in my community. I get to support the charities that are important to me around cancer and animal care.

My love for Stefanie is deeper than ever before and growing each day. My relationship with my son grows stronger each day. I am proud of what he and his wife have done at their young ages. My brother and I get to spend more time together than before.

I have the peace of mind knowing that I'm able to care of those I love and care about.

Life is rich and good!

Now it's time to write your letter of commitment to a new financial future. Remember, this truly isn't just about you but about the legacy you are living moment by moment as well as the ripple effect it will have on those you love, the causes that matter to you, and the generations to come.

PUTTING IT ALL TOGETHER: YOUR AFFLUENCE VISION ONE-SHEET

A vision is great, but we need to break it down into actionable milestones so you can make it a reality. Consider each of these six domains: (1) Family and Relationships, (2) Career and Business, (3) Health and Wellness, (4) Financial Security, (5) Lifestyle, and (6) Contribution and Legacy. Working backward from 10 years in the future, define where you need to be at the 5-year mark and what steps will get you there. Then do the same thing for the 12-month mark. This will make it easier to break your plan down even further into 90-day projects to move you closer to the vision you have. We're playing the long game here, and every step counts.

For example, if my financial goal is to own 10 rental properties in Southern California within 10 years, within the first 5 years, I'll need to have an evaluation process in place, own 5 properties, and have a management team for them. In the next 12 months, I'll need to hire a real estate agent, view two properties per week, and purchase one by the end of the year.

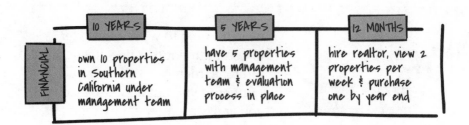

As another example, this time with my health domain: in 10 years, I feel vibrant, energized, and strong. In five years, I keep a healthy diet and live in a healthy environment. I've liberated myself from stress and friction in my life. I regularly get outdoors and do things that energize me. What I need to do in the next 12 months to make this a reality is to get my cancer under control through my diligent treatments and my work with my team of doctors. I learn to let go of stress and be more intentional with the stressors I allow myself to take on.

This is the process you'll use for all your domains, giving thoughtful consideration to each step required to make your 10-year vision a reality. This is a crucial move toward financial liberation and freedom—one that many people never take the time to complete.

Remember, when stating your goals, focus on what you want, not what you don't want. Keep your language positive and in the present tense, using phrases like *I am*, *I have*, and *I create*. Avoid words like *I will*, as they imply future tense. Make your goals measurable and set a deadline so you can track your progress and know when you've achieved success.

After brainstorming all the action steps and milestones necessary to achieve the goals in your contract, you can summarize them all in what I call an Affluence Vision One-Sheet. This one-page document will serve as a daily reminder of your vision and help you stay focused on your goals. Post it in a visible location and review it twice a day—every morning and evening. Share your goals with loved ones who can hold you accountable.

This is mine from a few years ago.

THE AFFLUENT VISION ONE SHEET ™

	10 YEARS	5 YEARS	12 MONTHS
CAREER OR BIZ	$1 million/ year to me working 100 days from anywhere	100 certified money mentors and 3 regions licensed	successful pilot, online program, affiliate launch & podcast show relaunch
RELATIONSHIPS	sharing & creating life & experiences built on richness with/for those I love	plan extended experiences with those I'm close to to deepen our connections	4 meaningful convos with friends/mo, quiet time with Stefanie weekly & vacays quarterly
HEALTH	vibrant, strong, cancer free, working out 6x/week, vitals great	healthy diet & environment, liberate from stress, outdoors & doing what I love	crush cancer by aggressive action, get to stressor zero
FINANCIAL	>$10 million investable assets, 100% leveraged income, still active biz cash flowing	mortgage free, $1 million fo investable assets & online biz cash flowing	refinance lower rate & cut 6 years, high converting funnel >$100 EPL, not "me" dependent biz
LIFESTYLE	create meaningful experiences, low stress and high joy sharing & serving	be intentional about causes and connections that matter, traveling qtrly, healthy living	finding 3 gratitude moments daily, outwardly expressed appreciation at least 1x daily

You can use this grid as a template for creating your own one-sheet. Note the blank row on the bottom, which is to allow you to add in other domains of your choosing, such as spirituality.

This process may seem overwhelming at first, but trust me, it's a game changer. As you make decisions in your life, ask yourself whether each choice brings you closer to or further from your vision. Always view your choices through the lens of your money purpose statement. By consistently aligning your actions with your goals, you'll be able to enjoy the process and stay on track. This powerful approach to goal-setting can transform your life, allowing you to live a life of affluence and fulfillment on your own terms.

ACTION ITEM

Boom—let's get your one-sheet completed now. This becomes your future on a page. It will act as a reminder when you start to lose sight of the vision. It will help hold you to your commitment, and it'll give you achievable milestones along the way to strive for.

Be sure to discuss your vision with your partner, family, or friends, and as you create a road map to achieve your goals.

Regularly revisiting and refining your vision will help you stay focused and aligned with your goals. I do this exercise regularly to this day. I used to do it quarterly, but now I do it once a year. Afterward, Stefanie and I sit down and talk about it. My son, Jeremy, and his wife, Kamie, do the same thing so they can both be on the same page for what they want, individually and together.

The idea of having money conversations with a romantic partner can be daunting for many people, but it's important to remember that it's only because we haven't been taught how to have them before. The only way you and your significant other can be on the same page about each other's goals and visions and understand each other's decisions is by talking about your visions and having clear plans on how to reach them.

For my client Corrine, the Affluence Vision conversations she had with her husband rekindled their entire relationship. They were champions for each other from the sidelines, but now they're moving forward as a team. In fact, after more than 20 years together, they just booked another honeymoon.

Corrine Acampora

 Hey Mel! Just wanted to drop you a line and let you know that your podcast and work has really sparked a lot of conversation between my husband and me that's been so good for us from not only a financial perspective but a relationship perspective. We realize that have two parallel success stories but have not fully integrated them after being together for more than 20 years. We've decided to break down the silos and really be team players for each other rather than rooting each other on from the sidelines. We both really love your take on family, money and entrepreneurship and how they need to work in harmony. Feels like after so long we had some sort of awakening. We even decided to go on a second honeymoon. :) thank you!🙏

Corinne and her husband are now bringing their kids into the conversations as well. They're saying, "Okay, let's buy into this vision as a family. How are the decisions we're making individually and together moving us closer to it?" Because then we're talking about achieving a vision; we're not judging someone for what they spent. So it's an easier conversation, and it's unifying. I give some tips in Appendices C and D to jump-start these money conversations between couples and with your kids.

As the late Stephen Covey, renowned author and speaker, wisely said, "Begin with the end in mind." By committing to this Affluence Vision process and your Affluence Plan, you're taking a powerful step toward creating the life you desire. This method has the potential to change lives, including your own. As you embark on this journey, remember that you have the power to shape your future—and it starts today.

Your Reality

Your situation can be seen as a problem or an opportunity, depending on what lens you choose to look through.

— MEL ABRAHAM

CHAPTER 7

GAUGING YOUR MONEY SITUATION TODAY

Your current truth is the springboard to a new financial future.

— MEL ABRAHAM

We've figured out your future—now it's time for us to take a deeper look into where you are today financially. From that, you can determine what your gap is.

Evaluating your reality can sometimes be eye-opening and even confronting for folks. I get it, and I want you to approach this new knowledge from the perspective of gaining awareness, not as a way to feel bad or guilty or to judge yourself.

Whatever got you here is the journey you were on in the past. You are on a new journey now, and things will change for you. And trust me, I've looked myself in the eyes plenty of times and come to grips with truths that at first were hard to accept. But in every case, once I did it, I was far more empowered and able to move and grow from it. You will be too.

To take control of your financial future, it's essential to have a clear understanding of some terminology and evaluate your income, expenses, assets, liabilities, and debt, as well as recognize that not all net worth is equally valuable. In this chapter, we'll dive into each of these so you have a solid understanding of where you stand financially and how each of these can impact your wealth and ultimately your path to financial freedom. By the end of this chapter, you'll be better equipped with the knowledge and tools to make informed decisions and create a solid financial foundation for your future.

Effectively, we are answering these three questions:

1. Where does my money come from, and where does it go? (income and expenses—net cash flow)

2. What do I own, and what do I owe? (assets and liabilities—net worth)

3. What do I have available to help me grow? (investable net worth)

ACTION ITEM — Pull up your bank accounts, credit card statements, and investment accounts for the last six months at least and come on back. Oh, and if you're worried what this exercise might reveal, then grab your favorite beverage and settle in.

INCOME: WHERE DOES YOUR MONEY COME FROM?

The first step in figuring out your money situation is to get clear on where your money is coming from. Income can be derived from various sources, including your job (salary), side hustles (profits), investments (interest, dividends, and gains), rental properties (net rent after expenses), or even other sources (residual payments, royalties, etc.).

It's essential to be aware of your various sources of income and their stability. For example, some sources may be consistent, like a salary, while others may be sporadic or seasonal, like freelance work. By understanding the nature of your income, you can better plan and budget for the future. So, mark each of the sources so you know if it's consistent, seasonal, or sporadic. This way it will be clear.

Once you have these numbers, you know what you have available to work with currently. We'll look at ways to increase these amounts later.

Make a list of all the sources that contribute to your income, and determine how much each source generates on a monthly basis.

EXPENSES: WHERE DOES YOUR MONEY GO?

Next, it's crucial to know where your money goes by tracking your spending. It's helpful to organize your expenses into two categories: short-term changeable costs and long-term fixed costs. Short-term changeable costs are those that can be adjusted quickly, such as groceries, entertainment, and travel expenses. Focusing on these costs allows you to make immediate adjustments to your spending habits. On the other hand, long-term fixed costs like your mortgage, rent payments, and other set bills are more difficult to modify in the short term. Recognizing the distinction between these two types of expenses can help you better manage your budget and prioritize financial adjustments as needed.

To get an accurate picture of your spending habits, track your expenses for at least one month. Organize them by short-term changeable costs and long-term fixed costs.

Once you've listed your expenses, go through each of them and decide if it's a need, a want, or should be canceled.

Remember, every dollar you save is a dollar that can be invested in your financial future and used to build your Money Machine.

Just so we're clear, a *need* is everything you need for your survival—things like food, clothing, shelter, medical, and reasonable transportation, and that's pretty much it. Everything else is a *want*. I can hear you now, but no, Netflix, mani-pedis, the latest technology, and things like these are not needs; they're wants. Now, before you get the pitchforks out because you think I'm grabbing the creamy, steaming oat-milk latte out of your hands, remember, I'm not telling you to do anything with your wants—yet. I'm simply asking you to list them and become aware.

Often, we're actually completely unaware of all our expenses and how things creep into our spending that we don't need or even use, let alone want. My job is to help you become aware, conscious, and deliberate with all you do around money. This will allow you to make your own decisions, and to do it fully informed.

Here's what I mean: Ethan is the 23-year-old that cuts my hair, and we're constantly talking about money stuff as he cuts. Recently I was sitting in the chair, and he mentioned that one of his good friends just spent $5,000 on a new watch.

"$5,000! Does he make a lot of money?" I asked.

He laughingly said, "Are you kidding? He's my age. No."

I was curious and asked what had made the friend buy a $5,000 watch at 23 years old.

"Because his other friends thought it was cool," he responded.

"Hmmm, 'cool' . . . can I do some math for you?" It was actually a rhetorical question, because I was going to do the math anyway. "Every dollar you put away in your twenties will turn into between seventy and eighty dollars by the time you're ready to retire. That means, had he invested the five thousand dollars instead, it could've turned into as much as four hundred thousand toward his financial freedom.

"So, what really happened is that spending this five thousand dollars in his present cost his future self four hundred thousand dollars to impress a group of guys that in all likelihood won't even be in his life in a handful of years."

Ethan was floored. "So everything I'm spending today is costing my future self eighty times as much in my future?"

"Heck yeah! You have the greatest wealth-building power *right now*."

"Oh man, I better get serious then. My life could be so much easier down the road!"

Now, I want you to hear me loud and clear on what I'm about to say.

I don't mind that people spend money. I don't mind if *you* spend it. Heck, Stefanie and I spend plenty of money and love really nice things. What I care about is when we spend money without understanding the true cost of the spending.

I just want you to be fully educated, empowered, and equipped to make conscious, aware, and intentional money decisions. If you're fully informed of the entire cost and are still 100 percent on board with it, then spend away, because you know exactly what the impact is.

ACTION ITEM Go back to your expenses, specifically all the "wants." Decide what to keep and what is no longer needed. Cancel all the things you no longer want.

You now have more money to allocate toward getting out of debt or building wealth or liquidity! We'll go deeper into how to do so when we talk about the Wealth Priority Ladder in Part III.

INCOME MINUS EXPENSES: NET CASH FLOW

An *income statement* summarizes your income and expenses on a single page so you have a clear snapshot of where you stand. It answers the first question we asked earlier: Where does my money come from, and where does it go? It's all about the cash flow coming in and detailing its sources and destinations. It helps you understand your income and spending/expenses, with the most basic equation being:

Income - Expenses = Net Cash Flow

Your goal is to find ways to increase income while simultaneously decreasing expenses to maximize cash flow. We'll discuss strategies for boosting income further in Part III.

ASSETS: WHAT DO YOU OWN?

Assets are anything you own that has value, such as real estate, vehicles, investments, and personal belongings. Make a list of your assets and determine their approximate value.

Keep in mind that not all assets are created equal. Some, like real estate and investments, can appreciate in value over time, while others, like vehicles, typically depreciate. Be careful here, because some things that you might think are assets really aren't. If something is a consumable, then it isn't an asset. In this context, *consumables* are things with utility but little to no lasting value, such as computers, phones, or clothing.

An asset, for our purposes, is something that goes up in value that you can use to pay for your living and lifestyle. There are two primary ways that you can do this: sell it for its value or get paid in some way for others to use it such as through rent. The classic example is a rental home. The key is to make sure that the cash flow that you receive is more than the expenses of owning it.

It's a common misconception that your primary residence is your most significant asset. While it may appreciate in value and is thus an asset, it doesn't generate cash flow unless you sell or rent it, making it a less effective wealth-building tool. Focus on building assets that have the potential to grow in value and contribute to your long-term financial success. These include stocks, bonds, income-producing real estate, and other assets like these.

 **ACTION ITEM** List out all the assets you have, an estimate of their current value, and the cash flow that you can generate from it.

LIABILITIES: WHAT DO YOU OWE?

Now let's look at the other side of the coin—*liabilities*, or debt. This is everything you might owe someone else, no matter what it's for. It includes any financial obligations such as loans, credit card balances, and mortgages, but it could also include unpaid taxes, medical bills, unpaid divorce obligations, and things like that.

Understanding your liabilities and debt is crucial to your ability to build wealth. It's also important so you can craft a strategic plan to pay them off. We'll talk more specifically on how to prioritize your debt plan in Part III and give you access to a free resource to help you make it a reality. But know that at some point in your financial journey, you'll want to be completely debt-free, because it takes a huge financial weight off your shoulders.

ACTION ITEM

Make a list of your liabilities, the amount of the monthly payment, and the interest rate (if one applies) and calculate the total amount of liabilities you currently have.

ASSETS MINUS LIABILITIES: NET WORTH

A *balance sheet* summarizes your assets and liabilities to answer the question: What do you own, and what do you owe? The financial equation looks like this:

$$Assets - Liabilities = Net\ Worth$$

Net worth represents what would be left after you pay all your debts and obligations. It's a snapshot of what you own (assets) and what you owe (liabilities). If you're not tracking this number, you're likely not building wealth and may struggle to achieve financial freedom. This actually is the foundation of building your Money Machine and the key to your path to financial freedom.

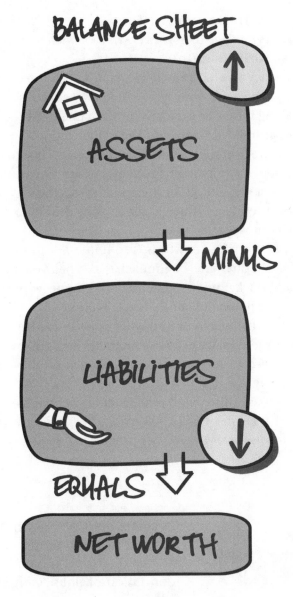

Think about it this way. If you buy a house for $500,000 and take out a mortgage for $400,000, you'd have an asset worth $500,000, a liability of $400,000, and a net worth of $100,000.

Hopefully, what we own is greater than what we owe. If not, we are what we call *illiquid*, or *insolvent*. This is what leads to bankruptcies. This can happen when we take on too much debt or the value of what you own goes down too much to where you owe more than what it's worth.

Insolvency is what caused so many foreclosures in the 2008 recession. Folks took on way too much debt because the lenders were making it easy to get loans. At the same time, the real estate values were inflated—so when the values dropped, people were left with more debt than value in the property. They couldn't even sell the property to pay off the debt, because the debt was more than what they could get for the property. It's the very reason you should be careful and strategic about using debt to make sure you do it the right way.

Also, this is why net worth is so important to track, whether on a monthly, quarterly, or annual basis. When you first start out, you should track it more frequently just so you get in the habit of checking the pulse on your financial health.

In fact, when you're setting your goals at the beginning or at the end of the year, we can set a financial goal similar to *I want to increase my net worth by* x *percent or* x *dollars* to set those milestones along the way.

You can use this goal to understand how your daily decisions will affect your net worth. Ask yourself, *Is this something that's going to increase my net worth, or is it going to decrease my net worth?*

ACTION ITEM

Calculate your net worth now. Commit to tracking it monthly, or at least quarterly, as you build the foundation of financial freedom.

INVESTABLE NET WORTH: WHAT DO YOU HAVE AVAILABLE TO HELP YOU GROW?

Let's go deeper into net worth. While your total net worth is a crucial metric, there's actually a more precise metric to consider when building your Money Machine—it's what I call Investable Net Worth. This is the only part of your net worth that has the ability to produce cash flows and support your Affluence Vision lifestyle. Here's the deal: from a financial freedom standpoint, only the assets that can fund your lifestyle should be considered as part of your Money Machine.

As I mentioned earlier, it's a common misconception that your primary residence is your most significant asset. While it may appreciate in value and is an asset by definition, from the perspective of cash flow and supporting your lifestyle, it isn't. It actually costs you money.

Now, I get it, you need a place to live, so I'm not saying your home has no value—just that it isn't considered as part of your Money Machine or Investable Net Worth.

With that in mind, then, your Investable Net Worth includes assets like 401(k)s, IRAs, stocks, bonds, and income-producing real estate as well as anything that can produce cash flow.

Calculate your investable net worth. Add up all the income-producing assets you own, subtract your debt, and arrive at a final figure. This number will help you track your progress toward building a Money Machine.

Your calculation could look a little something like this:

ASSETS	TOTAL NET WORTH	INVESTABLE NET WORTH
Cash	$10,000	$10,000
Stocks	$150,000	$150,000
Bonds	$50,000	$50,000
401K	$250,000	$250,000
Rental Property	$175,000	$175,000
Residence	$275,000	$0
Cars	$15,000	$0
Personal Items	$10,000	$0
TOTAL ASSETS	**$935,000**	**$635,000**
LIABILITIES		
Medical bills	$5,000	$5,000
Student loans	$45,000	$45,000
Mortgages	$200,000	$200,000
TOTAL LIABILITIES	**$250,000**	**$250,000**
NET WORTH	**$685,000**	**$385,000**

Focus on building assets that appreciate and are cash-flowing, such as real estate and investments, while minimizing depreciating assets, like vehicles, and eliminating high-interest debt.

Additionally, consider the liquidity of your assets. Liquid assets, like cash and easily accessible investments, provide flexibility in case of emergencies or unexpected expenses. Strive to maintain a healthy balance between liquid and illiquid assets to ensure both short-term financial stability and long-term growth.

When you combine the idea of increasing your net worth through maximizing your income and minimizing your expenses while acquiring assets to generate more cash flow, you get what I call the Affluence Cash Flow Matrix™.

CHAPTER 8

THE AFFLUENCE CASH FLOW MATRIX

Don't give up what you want most for what you want now.

— MEL ABRAHAM

Now we're going to put all the pieces I discussed in the last chapter into the Affluence Cash Flow Matrix framework, and I'll show you how they all work together.

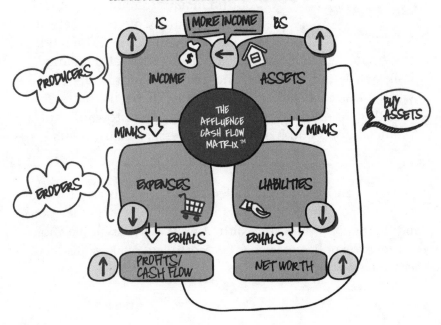

You want income that will produce cash flow so you can buy assets that will generate more income and further increase your net worth so you can do the cycle again. This is because in the process of buying the right assets, net worth goes up, income goes up, profits go up, and net worth goes up more. That is what's going to allow you to build a Money Machine.

Think about income and assets as Producers generating wealth, while expenses and liabilities are Eroders that drain your financial wealth. The wealth-building cycle involves using profits from Producers to buy more assets, which in turn increase your net worth and income, creating a Money Machine.

In the wealth-building cycle, profits generate cash flow, which you can use to purchase assets that create income and increase net worth. As your net worth grows, you can continue reinvesting in assets to further increase your wealth.

Taking Inventory and Moving Forward

ACTION ITEM

To gain a clear understanding of your financial situation, it's crucial to take inventory of your assets and liabilities. If you skipped the work in Chapter 7, do it now. Create a spreadsheet detailing your assets and liabilities, and calculate your total net worth. Track this information at least quarterly, preferably monthly, to ensure you're making progress toward your financial goals and making any necessary adjustments.

Once you have a clear understanding of your assets, liabilities, and net worth, it's time to evaluate your daily decisions and their impact on your wealth. Always ask yourself if a choice will increase or decrease your net worth, and make adjustments accordingly.

As you begin this journey toward financial freedom, it's imperative to be flexible. If you're not currently living the affluent lifestyle you desire, or you're struggling to make ends meet, it's time to get real with yourself and take action. Remember that the work you do now to better understand and take control of your financial situation is essential for achieving your goals. Don't settle for rough estimates or simply ballparking your needs; instead, be precise and specific, and plan for *both* your needs and wants.

Again, the choices you make with your money today should all be in service of the financial future you want tomorrow.

You may estimate that you need $20,000 per month to survive, but what if you're wrong? What if you need $30,000 per month? If you don't know the exact number, you may get there and discover you have one-third less than what you actually need. Or what if you don't need $20,000? Maybe you only need $10,000 and you stretch and stress yourself out over the years trying to build something more than you need. I totally get that this is a good problem to have as opposed to the alternative, but remember, the idea is that you live a rich life. A rich life is how you experience it and what you feel through it. Being stressed and stretched doesn't get you there—it just gets you hurt.

I remember on a warm summer day back in 2009, I was riding my mountain bike to the gym. I always loved the feeling of freedom I got when I flew down the hill with the wind blasting me in the face. But this ride was a little different. I didn't feel free. I was angry. I was distracted.

All of this would've been fine, except my shoelace got caught in the chain. As luck would have it, it happened at the steepest part of the downhill, which meant I was going my fastest. I don't really recall what happened next, but I must've clipped the brake, which turned my bike ride into a flight. Which was fine . . . until the landing. Yep, I stuck the landing. On my head, out cold, face down on the pavement.

I woke up to a nurse standing over me and a grade 4 concussion, no feeling on my right side, and the inability to speak clearly.

After a short stint in the hospital, I was sent home to finish recovering. One of my dearest friends came over to get me out of the house and take me to lunch. As we sat down at a little pastrami place we loved, he looked at me and asked, "How much is enough?"

I stared at him. Mind you, I'm still in a neck brace, stuttering and struggling to get the feeling back on my right side. "Dude, I just got out of the hospital from a bike accident that could've killed me, and you want to ask life's philosophical questions?"

He kept at it. "Seriously, how much is enough? Do you have any idea where your finish line is? You got on that bike angry, distracted, and with no real focus because you feel compelled to keep running as if that's going to satisfy you one day. The problem is, you have no idea where you're going or where your finish line is. That means you'll never know when you get there. Heck, it could already be behind you, but you're clueless about it.

"You'll heal from this accident, but if you don't take the time to understand what your 'enough' is and what it looks like for you, you'll get back on that bike angry, distracted, and running again. You'll crash and burn again . . . only next time could be worse. How much is enough?"

I know, *ouch*! But he was right. At that time, I was simply accumulating and achieving and acquiring with no rhyme or reason. I had assumed that at some point, I would just figure it out. But the reality is, I wasn't figuring it out because I never slowed down enough to define what I wanted my life to look like.

I mean really define it, in detail. Every aspect of what I wanted, without filtering or editing. Without worrying about how or judging—simply dreaming on an emotional level to know where I wanted to be and what mattered most to me.

You have to know what your finish line looks like. And let me be clear: I don't believe we are ever really finished. But we need to start with a vivid, compelling picture of where we're going.

This is why we did the work in the last section—so you have a better idea of the life you want to live and how much it may cost to live it. This approach will help you create a financial plan that supports the lifestyle you envision and, quite frankly, deserve.

As you work through this process after identifying your gap in the next section, remember that your current financial situation will determine your area of focus, and also that through the process, your situation will change.

The process works *if* you work the process.

Now that we've defined your starting point and your destination, what's left is the gap. This is going to become the wealth we need to create.

Your Gap

*Even imperfect action is action,
and action creates momentum.*

— MEL ABRAHAM

CHAPTER 9

THE FINANCIAL FREEDOM JOURNEY

Build a life, not an account.

— MEL ABRAHAM

Your financial future is built on the decisions you make today. Achieving financial freedom requires a shift in mindset from focusing on short-term gratification to long-term fulfillment. Many people get caught up in the pursuit of immediate pleasures and fail to consider the long-term consequences of their financial decisions. It also requires new actions, habits, and behaviors to make your dream your reality. It may not be easy, and you may have a steeper hill or a bigger boulder to push than others, but that doesn't make it impossible. And it certainly doesn't make it something to give up on, because the richness of your life and your legacy depends on it, and those you love are impacted by how you navigate this.

Understanding the difference between your current financial situation and your desired future is the first step toward bridging the gap. Remember, your past does not have to define you. The only thing separating you from the vision you painted for your life in the early chapters are a few steps to implement. So, let's get to some numbers so we can identify the gap and become clearer on what you're working toward.

If you're saying that you're not a math person, remember that your wealth is on the other side of this math problem. It's not that complicated. You'll do some simple adding, subtracting, and multiplying as you determine your current financial situation, define your financial future, and compare your financial goals to calculate the gap.

To identify your financial gap, follow these steps:

1. *Define your financial future*, and estimate the expected annual lifestyle costs.

2. *Calculate your ballpark number* by multiplying your expected annual lifestyle costs by 25. Your ballpark number is the investable net worth needed to achieve that financial future. (I'll explain why in the next section.)

3. *Determine your current financial situation* by assessing your assets, liabilities, net worth, and cash flow.

4. *Calculate your gap.* Subtract your ballpark number (future net worth) from your current net worth. This gives you a tangible number to work toward and help you measure your progress on your financial freedom journey.

DEFINE YOUR FINANCIAL FUTURE

Envision your desired future, taking into account your goals, values, and lifestyle. Consider factors such as your ideal retirement age, desired income, and the level of financial security you want to achieve.

If you got really detailed while crafting your Affluence Vision in Chapter 6, then you may already know exactly what net worth and monthly cash flow you need. If you need a little guidance, grab your journal and Affluence Vision One-Sheet now.

Once you have your expected annual lifestyle costs, you can calculate a ballpark number for the net worth you'll need to fund that vision of your future.

CALCULATE YOUR BALLPARK NUMBER

The 4% Rule is a widely used guideline that can help you get a starting ballpark target number to move toward. I say "ballpark" because you'll adjust the number specifically for your unique needs as you refine your vision and journey over time. I see it more as a rule of thumb than a rule. Nonetheless, it is a great place to start.

Financial advisor William Bengen[1] developed this rule of thumb in the early 1990s, and it has since become a popular guideline for retirement planning. He conducted extensive research on historical investment returns and concluded that regardless of market conditions, a 4 percent withdrawal rate would allow retirees to maintain their lifestyle for at least three decades.

In other words, the 4% Rule is meant for determining the "safe" amount you can withdraw from your retirement savings each year. If you withdraw 4 percent of your portfolio's value in the first year of retirement and then adjust this amount for inflation each subsequent year, your retirement savings should last for at least 30 years.

With this rule you can reverse engineer the ballpark number of the net worth you need to reach to allow you to withdraw 4 percent per year without draining your assets. The way to do that is simple: take the expected annual expenses to achieve your lifestyle and multiply them by 25.

CALCULATE YOUR GAP

You should have a comprehensive understanding of your current financial standing after following all the exercises in Chapter 7. So now it's time to calculate your financial gap by subtracting your ballpark number from your current net worth.

The process could look like this:

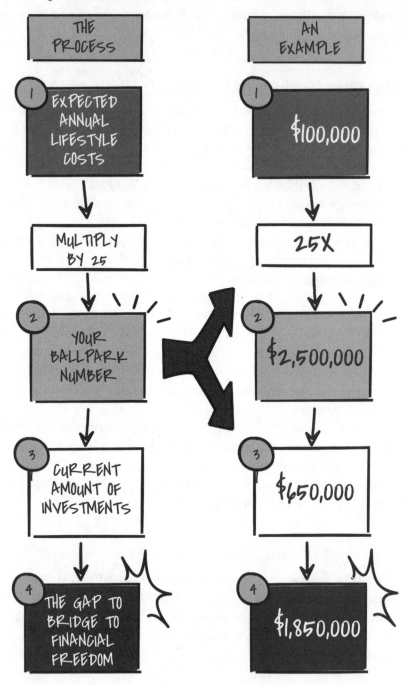

In this example of a financial gap, if we build $1,850,000 and add it to the $650,000 we already have, we get to $2,500,000. If that money is then able to earn 7 percent interest on average per year, we would be able to withdraw 4 percent of the $2,500,000 annually to get the $100,000 needed to cover our lifestyle expenses without eating up or eroding the $2,500,000. This is how a Money Machine works.

Remember, the 4% Rule is simply a starting point; it's important to remember that it's a ballpark that you'll refine with more precision as you grow and have more clarity and skills to work with.

ACTION ITEM

Time for some math. Following the four steps above, calculate your gap. Use your best estimate for your expected lifestyle costs as the starting point. This exercise is to inform you and equip you with an initial target for your financial freedom.

HOW YOUR FINANCIAL FREEDOM JOURNEY LOOKS

Now that you've identified your financial gap, it's time to embark on the journey toward financial liberation. This journey consists of four stages: stability, security, independence, and freedom. Too often, we look at the financial freedom number and freak out because it's so large and feels totally out of reach.

My number seemed out of reach too at one point. But when you break the journey into milestones and key steps, it makes it easier to move through. The path to close the gap as you head toward financial freedom will pass through four specific milestones. The milestone you're at determines where your focus will be moving forward.

THE FINANCIAL FREEDOM JOURNEY™

The first milestone is Financial Stability—which is having a firm financial foundation. It means having enough income from your Money Machine to cover your basic needs. This is your survival zone. It includes things like the roof over your head, medical care, food, clothing, and transportation. It's the necessities, not the niceties. But imagine how good it feels to know that your survival is covered. It becomes a calm, stable foundation that allows you to make even more powerful choices to move you to the next milestone.

The second milestone is Financial Security, which is about generating enough income from your Money Machine to cover all your survival needs *and* lifestyle niceties. Here, it's about your total current expenses. So throw Netflix, mani-pedis, and everything else you enjoy back in. At this milestone, you can continue to live your life at your current level without having to actually work.

The third milestone is Financial Independence, which is about having enough income from your assets to replace 100 percent of your current income.

Then there's the final milestone of Financial Freedom, the ultimate goal. This milestone is about your vision. Financial Freedom is about having a large-enough Money Machine to live the life you desire. It's about having the freedom to travel the world, pursue your passions, give back to your community, and create a legacy for your loved ones. It's about your Affluence Vision coming to life, and you living the legacy you're meant to create.

ACTION ITEM Write down your own milestone numbers! You've already done the exercises and Action Items in this book to calculate them, so grab your journal and flip to where you calculated the cost of your needs versus wants, your current monthly expenses, your monthly income, and your expected annual lifestyle costs. Write down these numbers and label them.

We all will go through these milestones on the journey to Financial Freedom. You may have already passed through one or more of these milestones, and if you haven't yet, you will. With each step, you'll be actively working to close your financial gap. Just stay on the path and follow the lessons I'm guiding you through in this book. One more thing . . . get excited for your new financial destiny, because it's coming.

CHAPTER 10

MONEY PERSONALITIES AND HABITS

*An apathetic attitude toward money
leads to a pathetic altitude of wealth.*

— MEL ABRAHAM

What you may not realize is that your relationship with money is deeply rooted in your personal money personality. Each person has a unique money personality that shapes how they interact with their finances. Just as personality assessments help you understand your default reactions and responses, your money personality reveals your go-to financial habits. By understanding these, you can be more aware and strategic in counteracting potential weaknesses and pitfalls while also magnifying your strengths to build a better financial future.

So, let's dig deeper into the four different money personalities I've seen in the folks I've worked with over the years. Understanding which one you most identify with can help you make better financial choices and navigate your financial journey with more confidence.

1. **The Saver** is like the superhero of financial prudence. They're cautious, disciplined, and always focused on building that financial safety net. Savers avoid debt like the plague and make sure they're always prepared for a

rainy day. But even superheroes have their kryptonite, and for Savers, it's their conservative nature that may hold them back from taking advantage of growth opportunities or enjoying the fruits of their labor. They never get to the richness of their life.

2. **The Spender** is all about living life to the fullest and enjoying the experiences money can bring. Spenders love the thrill of shopping and tend to make more emotional purchases. They live in the moment. However, sometimes their enthusiasm can get the best of them, leading to struggles with debt or living above their means. Spenders can benefit from embracing a little discipline, making more deliberate choices, and adopting a more strategic approach to managing their money.

3. **The Investor** is the financial adventurer, always seeking opportunities to grow their wealth. They know that money can work for them and are willing to take calculated risks to make that happen. Investors are knowledgeable about financial markets and love exploring new ventures. But sometimes they can get a little too focused on chasing returns and may overlook the importance of balancing risk and reward or attending to other aspects of their financial well-being. We'll talk more about risk later.

4. **The Philanthropist** is last but not least. These kind-hearted, compassionate souls find immense satisfaction in using their resources to help others and make a positive impact on the world. They're generous and caring, always looking for ways to give back. However, they might sometimes struggle to prioritize their own financial needs or set boundaries around their giving, which can impact their long-term financial stability.

I've spent my time in all four of these personalities at different points in my life. It's not that any one is better than another. We just need to understand when we're residing in them. I started out as more of a Saver; then I went to being an Investor. Now I'm a Spender and a Philanthropist, but I still have the Saver and Investor mindsets and tools.

Take a moment to reflect on which one of the personalities resonates most with you. Keep in mind that even though you may have traits from multiple categories, one usually takes the lead. Your money personality isn't set in stone; it can evolve and grow along with you. Be aware of your default habits and behaviors that arise as a result of your money personality, and adapt the strategies you'll learn in the upcoming sections so you'll be better equipped to navigate your financial journey with wisdom and confidence. We are about to dig deeper into your habits and how to create healthy money habits. For now, just raising your awareness goes a long way to changing them.

Last, as you look at the money personalities, think about your partner and their personality. Do you see the areas where you're similar, where you're different, and where there could be conflict if you aren't careful? Imagine how a Spender and a Saver would interact over time, possibly causing stress and friction.

These personalities often give rise to certain habits, and that's where the Habit Builder Framework™ comes into play.

THE HABIT BUILDER FRAMEWORK

As I've said repeatedly, your wealth building is driven more by your behaviors than your money. And your behaviors will be built on your habits. Implementing better habits is one of the best ways to start to close the gap that you've now identified so you can reach your financial goals (and, let's face it, any goal in your life).

Throughout our lives, many habits form unconsciously, just like the stories we create around money. We go through life on autopilot, not realizing that more than 40 percent of our actions are driven by habits.[1] The key to achieving financial success and freedom is to create habits intentionally, with a specific outcome in mind. So let's explore a framework to help you change your financial habits and set yourself on the path to financial freedom.

The Habit Builder Framework, my play on Charles Duhigg's Habit Loop from his book *The Power of Habit*, consists of four steps:

1. Define the root (trigger)

2. Define the reward

3. Eliminate expectation association

4. Curate a belief community

THE HABIT BUILDER ™

CURATE A BELIEF
COMMUNITY

ELIMINATE EXPECTATION
ASSOCIATION

DEFINE
THE REWARD

DEFINE THE
ROOT (TRIGGER)

1. TIME
2. LOCATION
3. EVENTS
4. EMOTIONS
5. PEOPLE

Step 1: Define the Root (Trigger)

The first step in creating habits that lead to financial success is identifying the root, or trigger, for the habit you want to change. The root is the thing that sets the conscious actions of a habit in motion. Similar to Charles Duhigg's cues, I identify five common triggers to consider.

The first root of a habit is time. Our actions and habits are often dictated by the time of day or the season. We can either be passively influenced by time, or we can use it as a deliberate trigger. For example, when I worked downtown, my colleagues would go to the clubs and bars straight from work like clockwork on Friday nights after getting paid. Think about this: time triggers can show up as shopping sprees, trips, or simply unconscious spending. Yet once you become aware of the trigger, it's much easier to stay conscious with your money choices. What if instead, paydays became a trigger to find new investment opportunities or causes that are exciting or speak to your passions? Imagine how much better you'd feel and how much longer lasting that feeling would be versus some fleeting, unconscious spend.

The second root is location. Curiously, certain places can evoke powerful responses. For instance, I find that walking into a hotel room triggers in me an urge to eat, even if I'm not hungry. I know it's weird, but that is the power of habits when we aren't conscious of them. Reflect on the locations that elicit responses in you. Are there places that consistently trigger a habit response? There's one I have to manage, especially when I'm traveling. I got into a habit of wanting to go out to a nice, expensive dinner whenever I land in a new town—which happens a lot because of my speaking engagements. I'm not sure why; maybe it's because I feel like I'm on vacation or something. But if you're doing that without thinking to the tune of $100 to $150 a meal, it adds up, and not in a good way. Another example with location as a trigger could be as simple as every time you go to pick up your mail next to the Starbucks, you run in to grab your latte and some snacks. This isn't an argument against the lattes but against the unconscious habit. By recognizing the power of location, we can intentionally use it as a trigger for change.

The third root revolves around events. These triggers can be either positive or negative and may even contribute to conditions like PTSD. Events can lead to emotional responses, such as receiving a paycheck and deciding to invest, or maybe getting up to greet your spouse when you hear the garage door open. By understanding event triggers, we can navigate them more effectively. A common time I see this happen is when people are planning for a trip, which then becomes the trigger for buying a whole new wardrobe. I know Stefanie and I have been guilty of this one for sure. By the same token, a positive trigger I have is that every major project payment I get, I make four allocations immediately—taxes, what I need for operations, celebrations, and investments. This is something called Leapfrog Funding that I teach my clients—which is when adding in lump sums causes your wealth to jump up and over your original anticipated target increases.

Emotions serve as the fourth root. Have you heard the term *retail therapy*? Well, that's the domain of the emotional spender. Our inner state can influence our actions, as seen in stress eating or shopping during times of anger or fear. Recognizing the role of emotions in our habits is crucial for creating positive change. By being aware of our triggers, we can shift them toward more constructive outlets. If you're an emotional spender or a stress spender, you could simply find a productive outlet when the trigger hits, like going to the gym or making a donation to a charity that matters. Especially with emotional triggers, there's some sort of need that's being served beyond the buying of something. The key is to find a better way to satisfy the need instead of using the swipe of a credit card.

Last, the fifth root is people. Our interactions with others can greatly impact our emotional state. Some individuals might evoke feelings of discomfort, while others bring joy and positive energy. Even our pets, like my dog, Budo, can bring a sense of peace and happiness. By understanding the influence of people in our lives, we can make conscious choices about the relationships we cultivate and the triggers we allow to shape our experiences. Think of partners where one might be a spender and the other gets triggered seeing the Amazon boxes show up on their doorstep daily. I had one couple that used spending as almost a game. When one would spend, the other felt the need to spend an equal amount to "stay even." First off, there was much more going on in that relationship than just poor spending habits, but they certainly didn't help.

None of this is intended to tell you not to spend but to make you aware of where unconscious habits can be eroding your money choices over time. By understanding the roots of these habits in your life, you can consciously create new habits that support your financial goals.

Step 2: Define the Reward

Once you've identified your key triggers, it's essential to define the reward you'll receive when you execute the right habit. This reward should be emotionally compelling and meaningful to you. For instance, if you're trying to curb impulse spending, your reward might be saving up for a special trip or focusing on something you've always wanted instead of some mindless impulse purchase.

Step 3: Eliminate Expectation Association

Be mindful of the decisions you make based on the expectations of others. Many times, we make financial decisions influenced by societal pressures or the actions of those around us. Even career decisions are often based on the expectations of others. To change your financial habits, it's crucial to make decisions based on your goals, values, and vision—and no one else's.

For instance, had I lived into the expectation of my career path as an accountant, I would have stayed the course in the firm to become a partner, which meant that I would continue to work late into the night on someone else's terms, not having any control over my time or making the level of impact I get to make today. I would not have had the chance to travel to speak (or for fun) or to serve and help my clients reach their fullest financial potential and impact. In short, I would have been miserable at the core but would have done it anyway. Why? Because that was expected of me. How many times do we find ourselves doing things because others expect us to instead of by choice?

Step 4: Curate a Belief Community

Surround yourself with individuals who understand and support your financial goals. This may include coaches, mentors, or like-minded friends who hold you to a higher standard and encourage you to stay on track. Your belief community should not only provide positivity but also challenge you to grow and stay committed to your financial objectives.

To start consciously crafting your financial habits, consider the following questions. Your answers to them will become clearer as you go through this book:

1. What habits do I need to support my financial goals?
2. Who do I need to help me on this journey?
3. Who do I have to be to have the things I want?
4. Am I doing the things that a person who has what I want would do?

As you reflect on these questions, remember that the underlying motivation for change is your *why*. If your reason for pursuing financial freedom is strong enough, you'll be more likely to create and maintain the habits necessary for success.

To begin your journey toward financial freedom, identify one money habit you identified in the prior Action Item that you can start within the next seven days. This could be as simple as: *This week, I'm going to check my balances once and find a way to reduce my spending by x dollars.*

Schedule this habit on your calendar and commit to taking the first step. By focusing on creating new habits, you'll shift your behaviors and, ultimately, your financial results. No matter your current circumstances, it's never too late to change your financial habits and move closer to financial freedom.

As you go through the lessons and tactics in this book, you'll be adding more and more good money habits to your list.

In continuing on your financial journey, you'll learn to periodically reassess your money situation to ensure you're staying on track and making progress toward your goals. When you take the time to evaluate and understand your financial life, you'll be better prepared to navigate the challenges and opportunities that lie ahead.

By doing this groundwork, you'll also be well prepared to embrace the wealth-building strategies laid out in Part III of this book.

Part III

CREATE THE JOURNEY

People create wealth by owning assets that
appreciate or create/earn other assets.

— MARK CUBAN

Let's look at how far you've come to get to this point. We first broke down the barriers that can get in the way of your financial freedom journey. These show up in the form of excuses, stories, and even fear, but now you have the tools and tactics to keep those under control so you can move beyond them.

You spent the time actually building out a vivid Affluence Vision and Affluence Plan for your life so you would know more specifically where you want to go with your money journey. You reduced that down to a one-sheet that breaks your path down into milestones so you can stay on track and keep your vision in front of you in a compelling and easy way.

Then you dug into where you are today with your money: where your money is coming from, where it goes, what you own, and what you owe. This allows you to understand the impact of net worth, investable net worth, the Affluence Cash Flow Matrix, and the four Wealth Drivers that will make up your Money Machine.

With the foundation of where you are today and the vision for where you want to go tomorrow, you were able to understand and calculate the gap between the two points. This is what you need to build to get to where you want to be financially. Filling this gap is the key to building the Money Machine you need, and the Money Machine is the key to your financial freedom.

So now you may be saying, "Great, I know where I am and where I want to go. But, Mel, *how* do I get there?" Not to worry; that's what we're doing in this section. I'm going to break down the process for the way I want you to allocate your money as you move through the financial journey toward freedom.

In Part III, we're going to walk step-by-step through the three pillars of your Money Machine—Earn, Grow, and Protect. With these three phases, we're aiming for three critical outcomes: lasting wealth, enduring freedom, and a living legacy. We'll delve into the nuts and bolts of constructing this machine by learning how to optimize your earnings (the fuel), transform those earnings into assets and grow them (the vehicle), and protect them from loss (the shield).

The first two parts of this book were about building the foundation and the framing of your wealth. In this section, we'll be doing the finishing work and making all your work come to life. Are you ready? Let's do this!

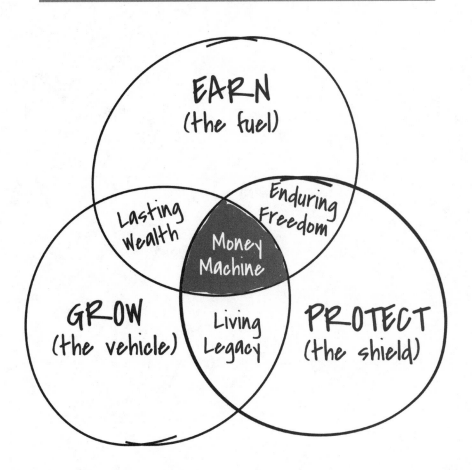

Earn

It's not simply about keeping what you make but multiplying what you make.

— MEL ABRAHAM

CHAPTER 11

UNLOCKING YOUR EARNING POTENTIAL

Dollars follow value, not effort or hours!

— MEL ABRAHAM

VALUE VS. INCOME

When people attempt to boost their income, the common misstep is prioritizing income itself. Instead, you should concentrate on enhancing your value, which will eventually result in increased income.

Rather than fixating on your present earnings, take a moment to envision a larger goal beyond your current situation. Embrace your true earning potential by understanding the distinction between value and income, and recognize how emphasizing value creation can ultimately lead to greater earnings and growth.

Income is the money you receive for your work, whether through a salary, hourly wages, or business profits. It's the tangible outcome of your labor and often the primary focus for many people when they think about their financial lives.

Value, on the other hand, refers to the worth you create for others. This could be in the form of products or services you provide, the knowledge or expertise you share, or even the positive impact you have on the lives of others. People pay for the value of the solutions you provide. Consistently creating and delivering value can lead to increased income over time.

Here are six reasons why focusing on value is so important in your financial freedom journey:

1. **Recession-proofing.** During times of uncertainty or recession, the people who not only survive but thrive are those who have a distinct value to offer the world. When you focus on value, you bring certainty to your earnings. With certainty in your earnings, you become somewhat immune to the economic swings that impact the folks who have not elevated their value and differentiated themselves. If you want a recession-proof life, control your earning ability by controlling and elevating your value.

2. **Exchange economy.** Like it or not, the level of compensation follows value, not time or labor. People will buy when they perceive the value of what they receive is greater than the value of what they give up in return. Focusing on increasing your value ultimately results in more income.

3. **Differentiation.** By concentrating on creating value, you set yourself apart from others in your field or industry. This differentiation can lead to increased demand for your products or services and, consequently, higher income. This moves you from transactional to more relational.

4. **Long-term sustainability.** A value-driven approach ensures that you're not just chasing short-term financial gains. Instead, you're building a solid foundation for long-term success and wealth accumulation.

5. **Adaptability.** Focusing on value allows you to be more adaptable in an ever-changing economy. By continuously seeking to improve and provide more value to others, you can pivot and adjust your offerings as needed to stay relevant and prosperous.

6. **Personal fulfillment.** Pursuing value creation is often more fulfilling than just chasing income. By making a positive impact on others, you're not only improving your financial situation, but also enriching your life and the lives of those you serve.

To incorporate the concept of value versus income into your financial freedom journey, consider the following steps:

1. **Identify your unique value proposition.** Determine what you do best and how you can provide exceptional value to others. Your unique value proposition is more powerful and compelling when it aligns with your passions, skills, and experiences.

   Let's say you were someone who loves managing projects. Your unique value proposition could look something like this:

   I'm all about making things happen. As an experienced project manager, I've got a track record of delivering projects on time and under budget. But what really sets me apart is my unique blend of leadership, strategic thinking, and technical expertise. I'm someone who not only knows how to get things done but also how to communicate effectively and build strong relationships with everyone involved. I'm passionate about delivering results that exceed expectations.

2. **Develop a plan to enhance and deliver your value.** Once you've identified your unique value proposition, create a plan to improve and share it with others. This may involve honing your skills, acquiring new knowledge, or expanding your network.

3. **Align your value creation with your financial goals.** Ensure that your value-driven approach is in line with your financial objectives. This could mean charging premium prices for your exceptional services or products, or seeking opportunities to monetize your expertise in multiple ways.

4. **Continuously assess and refine your value.** Regularly evaluate the value you're providing and make adjustments as needed. Stay attuned to market trends, customer feedback, and new opportunities to ensure that you're always delivering maximum value.

5. **Appreciate your value.** This is one of the most important factors: If you don't appreciate the value you bring, others won't either. Find the value in you and own it, ask for it, and live into it.

The fact is that shifting your focus from income to value creation will actually grow your income through getting paid more. It will help you accelerate your path through the four levels of your financial journey (stability, security, independence, and freedom). This approach not only leads to greater financial rewards but also promotes personal growth, satisfaction, and a meaningful, fulfilling life.

 Write out your unique value proposition. Take the time to examine the value you bring as well as the source of that value. Consider whether those you work with or for see your value. If they do, then make sure you're getting paid at the level consistent with the value you provide. If they do not, it is on you to show it to them at a level that they will pay for.

THE SKILL UP, VALUE UP APPROACH

The world is constantly changing and with it, the skills and expertise that are in demand. By investing in yourself and continually improving your skills and abilities, you can position yourself for success and thrive in an ever-changing and competitive marketplace.

The Skill Up, Value Up Approach is powerful because it offers key benefits, including increased earning potential by becoming more valuable in your field, which leads to better job opportunities, promotions, or entrepreneurial success. This strategy also ensures job security, as continuously improving your skills makes you indispensable to employers or clients, thus reducing susceptibility to job loss or market fluctuations. Moreover, personal and professional growth fosters confidence, a sense of accomplishment, and a passion for your work, leading to greater success and career satisfaction. Finally, building expertise enables the creation of assets like books, courses, or other intellectual property, generating leveraged income that contributes to your overall financial freedom.

You can skill up and increase your value through a variety of methods. Here are some examples:

- **Formal education.** A degree or certification in a field can provide a solid foundation of knowledge and skills that are valuable in the job market. This can involve attending college or university, vocational school, or specialized training programs.

  According to *The College Payoff*, a report from the Georgetown University Center on Education and the Workforce, those with a bachelor's degree can earn as much as 75 percent more than those with just a high school diploma.[1] Finishing college puts workers on track to earn a median of $2.8 million over their lifetimes, compared with $1.6 million for those with only a high school diploma.

- **On-the-job training.** Many employers offer on-the-job training programs or professional development opportunities that can help employees gain new skills and advance their careers. This can involve attending workshops, taking courses, or working closely with mentors or more experienced colleagues.

  One of the cool ways to learn more and grow more is to *ask* for more. Here's what I mean: Many companies are willing to pay for or send you to special training in return for your commitment to stay with them. It becomes a win-win situation: They get a more skilled employee, and you can make the case to get paid more for your skills. And now they have the ability to increase their employee retention or attraction for new recruits, because on-the-job training becomes a benefit.

  Here's an interesting but disturbing stat: According to an International Foundation of Employee Benefit Plans study, fewer than 5 percent of employees take advantage of these educational/skill-up opportunities. If you have access, why not take advantage of it?[2]

- **Self-directed learning.** In today's digital age, there are countless resources available online for you to learn new skills and knowledge on your own. This can include watching educational videos, reading articles or books, or participating in online courses or webinars. (Be sure to visit MoneyMachineResources.com.)

    I'm not only a believer in self-education but a product of it. One of the mistakes I see people make is believing that once they have a degree or certificate, they are done with their education. The reality is that your degree or certificate is just the beginning, and your ability to increase your value is through the cultivation of your knowledge or skills throughout your life. Think about it this way: My degree and certificates were all financial and accounting related. That only got me to a certain level of value. But I quickly realized that to raise my value to a whole new level, I needed additional skills like communication, persuasion, negotiation, speaking, marketing, leadership, and coaching. I learned (and continue to learn) all of these through self-directed platforms, courses, and masterminds.

    No matter where you are or whether you have a degree, your access to new skills and training is far easier and more affordable than it has ever been, given the online resources we all have at our fingertips.

- **Networking.** Building a strong network of professional contacts is invaluable for expanding your knowledge and skill set. By connecting with others in your industry or field, you can learn about new opportunities, gain insights into emerging trends or technologies, and build relationships that can lead to new collaborations or job opportunities.

- **Volunteer work.** Volunteering can be a great way to gain new skills and experiences while also giving back to your community. By taking on volunteer roles that align with your interests and goals, you can develop new skills and gain valuable experience that can be applied to your professional life.

Here are some strategies to help you effectively Skill Up, Value Up for your financial freedom:

- **Identify areas for improvement.** A self-assessment will help you determine which skills to focus on to maximize your value. Assess your current skill set and determine the areas where you can grow or improve. Consider the skills most in demand in your industry, and prioritize those that can significantly impact your earning potential.

- **Set clear skill-development goals.** Establish clear, achievable goals for enhancing your skills. Break down these goals into smaller milestones and create a timeline for achieving them.

- **Pursue continuous learning.** Invest in your education by attending workshops, courses, or seminars; reading books; or listening to podcasts in your field. Embrace lifelong learning and remain open to new ideas, methods, and technologies. This investment in yourself will pay off in the long run by boosting your value in the market.

- **Seek mentorship and guidance.** Surround yourself with knowledgeable and successful individuals in your field. Attend industry events, join professional organizations, and engage with mentors who can offer guidance and support. Mentors can help you navigate challenges, avoid pitfalls, and accelerate your growth.

- **Practice and refine your skills.** Apply your new skills in your daily work, and seek out opportunities to practice and refine them. Consistent practice will help you master your craft and increase your value.

- **Network strategically.** Connect with like-minded professionals who share your passion for growth and value creation. Networking can open doors to new opportunities, collaborations, and knowledge exchange, ultimately benefiting your financial liberation journey.

- **Showcase your skills and value.** Highlight your skills, expertise, and accomplishments in your resume, portfolio, or personal brand. Demonstrating your value to potential employers or clients can open doors to new opportunities and higher earnings.

- **Evaluate and adjust.** Regularly review your progress toward your learning goals and assess the value you provide. Adapt your approach as needed to ensure you stay on track and remain proactive in the skills necessary to take you to where you want to go.

By committing to the Skill Up, Value Up Approach, you'll be better equipped to navigate the ever-changing professional landscape and increase your earning potential. This proactive approach to personal and professional growth will not only bring you closer to financial freedom but also provide you with a greater sense of fulfillment and purpose in your work.

ACTION ITEM Pick one of the strategies from the list and break it down into the next steps you need to take. For example, if you decide to network strategically, the next step may be to research new conferences in your field. Brainstorm ideas, and put at least one on your calendar as a commitment to following through.

Hopefully, this sets the stage for you to see possibilities to increase your earnings and income. Obviously, there are many more ways, like side hustles or doing independent gigs part-time. The most important thing to take away from this section is that by increasing your value to others, you increase your earning potential. By increasing your earning potential, you accelerate your path to building your Money Machine.

Now you may be asking, "But, Mel, what do I do with the money I'm making?"

Well, I'm so glad you asked, because that's where the Wealth Priority Ladder comes in. It's your instruction manual for what to do with each dollar and when.

CHAPTER 12

THE WEALTH PRIORITY LADDER

There is no first place or last place in life.
There's only your place.
Define it. Own it. Live it.

— MEL ABRAHAM

Imagine for a moment that you have 20 new employees you just hired, all starting at the same time. (I know, it's stressful already!) They show up, and you have them in the conference room at the office to do their introduction and onboarding. It might go something like this:

"Hey there, y'all, welcome to our company. I'm so glad you're here. We work a little differently from what you're used to. None of you have job descriptions. None of you have titles. None of you even have a specific place you should be. I'm not going to give you any specific goals. But together, I want us to create a successful business, build more profits, and make a lot of money so we can build wealth too."

Would you ever run a company this way? Not likely!

Let me ask you another thing: If you did that, how successful do you think the company would be? Do you think it would hit its goals? How long do you think a company like this would last?

It'd be a total disaster.

But the reality is that most people do exactly this with their money! Every dollar you make or bring in needs to have a specific job description and role in your financial journey. It's what I call a Cash Resource Plan. When you decide what each dollar is in your life to do, you'll have all your employees working toward the common goal of building your Money Machine.

One of the tools we use to help you with that is called the Wealth Priority Ladder. This is the process for deciding what every dollar should be doing.

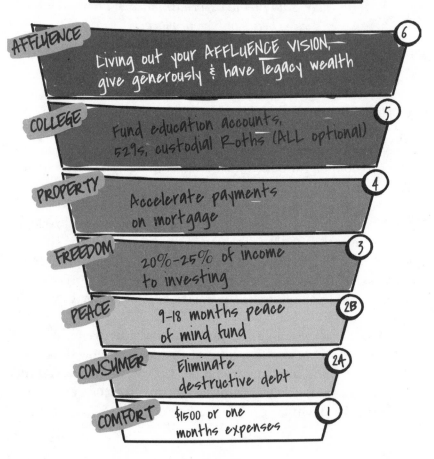

THE WEALTH PRIORITY LADDER ™

AFFLUENCE — Living out your AFFLUENCE VISION, give generously & have legacy wealth — 6

COLLEGE — Fund education accounts, 529s, custodial Roths (ALL optional) — 5

PROPERTY — Accelerate payments on mortgage — 4

FREEDOM — 20%–25% of income to investing — 3

PEACE — 9–18 months peace of mind fund — 2B

CONSUMER — Eliminate destructive debt — 2A

COMFORT — $1500 or one months expenses — 1

This is your recipe for wealth. When you're baking a cake, a recipe tells you not only what ingredients you need but also the specific amounts and the order in which to add the ingredients to the mix.

Well, the Wealth Priority Ladder does the same thing but for your money. We'll work through each of the levels from the bottom up. Just remember that, like a recipe, if you've got the ingredients wrong, in the wrong amounts, or in the wrong order, the end result will likely not be what you wanted . . . so follow the recipe. This is your Money Machine recipe.

PHASE 1: BUILDING AN UNSHAKABLE FOUNDATION

The Ladder is broken down into three-plus phases of focus. The first phase is about building an unshakable foundation.

Step 1: Establish a Comfort Fund

The first step in this phase is to build a Comfort Fund of at least one month's expenses or $1,500, whichever is greater. This is not a standard "emergency fund" but simply something to have in place to keep you from having to go into bad debt if something unexpected happens.

A recent Bankrate.com study showed that 44 percent of folks could not cover an unexpected expense of $1,000 or more.[1] This step is to keep you from being a part of that statistic. It's meant to cover things like a transmission that goes out, a repair you didn't plan on, a medical expense, or a deductible you hadn't thought about.

So your first dollars allocated should be to fund this step. Some clients look for things they can sell on Facebook Marketplace, Craigslist, or eBay to knock this out right away. Once you have this step fully funded, you can move to the next two steps—which should actually be done at the same time. That's why they're noted as *a* and *b*.

Step 2A: Eliminate Destructive Debt

I'm not one of those who believes all debt is the devil. I think there is destructive debt and productive debt. Now, let me be clear: At some point, I'm going to want you to be fully debt-free to eliminate the burden of payments from your cash flows. Whether the debt is productive or destructive, *all* debt shares these two characteristics:

1. **Debt costs you.** When you take on debt, there's a cost to it in the form of interest. That interest burden can get heavy, especially if you're in a rising interest-rate environment.

2. **Debt stresses you.** No matter the type of debt, having the obligation hanging over your head creates stress. It stresses your finances for sure, but it also stresses you psychologically.

So with that understanding, here's how I differentiate the two types of debt. Productive debt is that which will increase your net worth and/or cash flow because you're using it for investments and other assets that will build your Money Machine. Destructive debt doesn't increase your net worth or cash flow; it consumes it. Typically, this debt is for wants (lifestyle and consumables), not assets.

Any debt we carry on credit cards to pay for our regular living is destructive debt. Putting any lifestyle costs such as TVs, trips, or even clothes on credit cards that you pay interest on means that you are robbing your future to live today. Most consumables should not be paid for with loans or credit cards. A vehicle would be an exception to this rule, but it must be no more than 7 percent of your income and paid off in no more than 36 months (not the 72 months the salespeople are selling you on).

I want you to avoid and get out of all of your destructive debt as much as possible, because that's how most find themselves in a deep financial hole they can't get out of.

In this step, it's important to put yourself on a specific debt-payment plan. There are two popular methods to consider:

1. **Debt Avalanche.** Focus on paying off the debt with the highest interest rate first while continuing to make minimum payments on your other debts. Once the highest-interest debt is paid off, move on to the next highest-interest debt, and so on. This method minimizes the amount of interest you'll pay over time.

2. **Debt Snowball.** Focus on paying off the smallest debt first while continuing to make minimum payments on your other debts. Once the smallest debt is paid off, move on to the next smallest debt, and so on. This method provides quick wins, which can be motivating and help build momentum.

Choose the method that resonates with you, and commit to following your plan consistently. If you want help with this, I have a free tool that can schedule out your payments. You can find the Debt Breakthrough Calculator on the Money Machine Resource page at MoneyMachineResources.com.

Step 2B: Set Up Some Peace of Mind

Some people call this sum an emergency fund, but I call it a Peace of Mind Fund. I'm more conservative than most and believe that three to six months' worth of living expenses saved is not enough. I think you should have 9 to 18 months of expenses put away in a high-yield cash account that's fully insured, completely liquid, and without fees. I want you to have liquidity to sustain you through a prolonged difficult time if you need it.

Now, before you start in on me about how much you're losing to inflation, remember that each dollar has a job. The job of these dollars is to keep you safe and sane, not make you rich.

Putting Steps 2A and 2B Together

So, here's how to use Steps 2A and 2B: split the money you have to allocate between your debt payment plan and the Peace of Mind Fund.

Here's what this could look like: After you've created your Comfort Fund and paid the minimums on your debt, you have $1,000 a month. You'll split the $1,000 between your debt pay-downs, your Peace of Mind Fund. The money should be divided based on your priorities, not necessarily evenly.

PHASE 2: GROWING YOUR WEALTH AND MONEY MACHINE

At this point you have a comfort fund in place, you're on a destructive-debt paydown plan, you're building your Peace of Mind Fund. Once you've completed either paying off your debt *or* fully funding your Peace of Mind Fund.

Your freedom is built in this phase! Let's take a look.

Step 3: Invest and Grow

Now it's time to get 20 to 25 percent of your income invested. If you are younger and have a longer runway, you might be able to push this percentage slightly lower, to around 15 percent. But if you're later in life and haven't been building your wealth, you may need to push it to as much as 30 percent.

Now there are a whole host of accounts and places you can put your money like 401(k), IRAs, SEP IRAs, Roth IRAs, HSA, and ESPP. Then where does saving for a house or other big purchases come in?

I know it's confusing. Let's break down this step into its own set of priorities of where to put your money first and then next. Start from the bottom of this list and work your way upward.

Alternatives

Real Estate

Brokerage

Mega Backdoor

Backdoor Roth

HSA

401k Max

Roth IRA (maybe)

ESPP

401k Match

Free or Discounted Money

Your first priority will be to take advantage of any free money or discounted investments available to you. Here's what I mean:

- **401(k) match**: If your employer has a 401(k) where they match a portion of your contributions, this is literally free money. For instance, if they match up to the first 4 percent of your salary contributed, you'd effectively be getting an immediate additional 4 percent—a 100 percent return.

- **ESPP (employee stock purchase plan)**: Some companies have a stock purchase plan that allows employees to buy company stock at a discount from what others could buy it for on the stock exchange. The discounts typically range from 10 to 15 percent. For instance, my wife works for a company that has an ESPP with a 15 percent discount, so she can purchase $100 worth of stock for $85. Not a bad deal.

  Sometimes there are strings attached to the purchase plan that limit when and how much stock you can sell. Plans that are fully liquid have no such restrictions; you could buy at a discount and immediately sell the stock for a gain. Either way, it is another way to access free or discounted money.

Tax Advantaged or Deductible Accounts

- **Roth IRA**: These retirement accounts are restricted to those under a certain income threshold and have a yearly limit on contributions. If you are eligible, this should be your next priority.

  While you do not get a tax deduction for your contributions as with a 401(k), the beauty behind this account is that when you withdraw the money

at retirement age, all of it is tax-free. These accounts
are especially powerful for those that are younger
and in lower tax brackets as your account value grows
exponentially completely tax-free. Also if you are in
a lower tax bracket (below 25 percent), the tax-free
growth will be more valuable than the tax deduction
you might get.

- **401(k) max:** Once you've fully exhausted your free
  money and are maxing out your Roth IRA, you can
  come back to your 401(k). Contributions lower your
  taxable income, although you do need to pay taxes
  on withdrawals in retirement. Now is the time to go
  beyond just getting the employer match; max it out
  if you can. The maximum contribution limits can
  change every year.

  Now here is an interesting nuance to consider.
  Some 401(k)s are set up similarly to Roths. In
  other words, you would not get any tax deduction
  for the money you contribute but the growth on
  the contribution would be completely tax free at
  retirement. The cool thing about this is that the
  normal Roth IRA income and contribution limits
  do not apply. So if you are a high-income earner,
  this is a way for you to enjoy Roth benefits through
  your 401(k).

- **HSA (health savings account):** This is another
  account that may not apply to everyone, but when it
  does, boy, is it powerful. To open one, you must have
  a qualified high-deductible health plan. The money
  you put into an HSA is tax deductible or pre–tax (if
  made by payroll deduction). You make investments
  just like with any other investment account, but
  the growth is tax-free and withdrawals for qualified
  medical expenses are also completely tax-free.

This is where the real power comes in and how we guide our clients to use them. The IRS doesn't tell you *when* you need to take out the money to reimburse yourself for medical expenses. This means that you could leave the money in the account and save the medical receipts for years or even decades. But why would you do that, you ask? Reimbursing yourself later allows you to enjoy years of tax-free growth on the cost of that expense!

Let me put some numbers to this so you see what can happen. As of this writing, the current HSA yearly contribution limits for a family are $8,300. Let's assume you contribute that over the next 5 years for a total of $41,500. But instead of withdrawing the money to pay medical expenses in the year you had them, you invest the money and let it grow for 10 years after you stopped contributing. Assuming an average 8 percent return, the account would then be worth $105,124—well above the $41,500 you contributed.

Now when you need the money for whatever reason, you can dust off the old medical bills and reimburse yourself completely tax-free. For instance, after submitting $10,000 worth of receipts, you would not only be reimbursed for what you paid but also still have over $95,000 in the account. Not a bad way to go.

Another benefit is that after the age of 65, you can treat an HSA like a regular IRA account and withdraw money without penalty, even without documented medical expenses. However, you'd pay taxes on the withdrawals.

This strategy is highly dependent on personal circumstances. Those with complex medical needs will likely not benefit from the tradeoff of needing to pay all the costs incurred with a high-deductible health plan.

* * *

The following are powerful ways to build your wealth but more complicated. Always work with a good advisor to make sure you use these methods correctly.

- **Backdoor Roth:** While the term *backdoor* makes this strategy sound suspicious, a backdoor Roth is 100 percent legal. Since there are no income limitations when you convert a regular IRA to a Roth IRA, this method is used by those who exceed the income limitations that direct Roth contributions have.

  The way this works is that you would make a non-deductible, regular IRA contribution. You leave the amount contributed in cash for a few days, then convert it to a Roth. Once it is converted, you can invest the money.

  Now, there are some limitations here. Once the conversion is made, you must leave the money for at least five years. Also, it might become more complicated and less advantageous if you have other IRAs. You should talk to an advisor about your personal circumstances before trying to use this strategy.

- **Mega Backdoor Roth:** This strategy is another way to bypass the income limitations for the Roth IRA and can be valuable for high-income earners. It allows you to put close to $70,000 combined into your 401(k) between your contributions, your employer match, and your after-tax contributions. To utilize it, you must have a 401(k) plan that allows for "after tax" contributions and either allows an in-plan conversion or an in-service distribution. Many of the newer plans have these provisions automatically.

Here's how this works. At this stage you will have maxed out your regular 401(k) contributions and now are looking to put more money away. You make after-tax contributions to the 401(k), then leave the money in cash. After a few days you can do an in-service distribution or an in-plan conversion to convert those after-tax contributions you made to Roth.

Traditional Accounts and Investing

At this point, you have taken maximum advantage of any free money or discounted money available to you and used all of the tax advantaged accounts to maximize your benefits. Now we can look at other, more traditional accounts or investing.

- **Brokerage**: This is what most people think about when it comes to investing. Opening a traditional account at a brokerage like Schwab, Fidelity, Vanguard, or other discount brokers will allow you access to a good population of investments, ETFs, and index funds. (We will go into more detail on these in the next chapter.) You want a low-fee broker so you keep most of the money in your pocket, not theirs.

- **Real estate**: It is at this stage that real estate becomes a possible investment option for some people. I know that this may not be a popular opinion, but hear me out on this.

  The Wealth Priority Ladder is meant to optimize how you allocate your money and investing to maximize your potential for long-term success while reducing the potential risks and hazards to your wealth. Don't get me wrong, I love real estate. It is a great asset for investing in *at the right time* in your journey. I believe that time is once you've built a critical mass to your portfolio, and you have the liquidity it takes should a real-estate investment go bad.

Here's what I mean: If you have $50,000 to invest and you start with real estate, you will likely be able to buy only one property. All your eggs are in one basket, so if that property has any issues like unplanned repairs, extended vacancies, or even a nonperforming tenant who you need to evict, not only do you not have the cash flow you planned but also you're spending money. In many cases, the property would be leveraged, which then requires you to continue to make the payments on the loan with no money coming in. Finally, getting in or out of real estate is not as easy as selling investments in the stock market. It takes more market time and has substantially more costs.

It is for these reasons I want people to have enough liquidity and assets to carry real-estate assets before they start investing in it.

Alternative Investments

- **Alternatives**: Alternative investments refer to financial assets that do not fit into the conventional categories of stocks, bonds, and cash. These can include a wide range of investments such as syndications, commodities, hedge funds, private equity, cryptos, and collectibles, among others.

  Although some of them have the potential for greater returns than more conventional investments, they aren't without their risk and issues. Most often, they are illiquid and hard to get out of. Many of them do not have the same level of transparency, reporting, and investor protections as the conventional investments have. This is why it is typically the last category of investing that I have people look at. (And even then, it will not typically be a large percentage of their investments.)

Planning for Large Purchases in Step 3

Around this time, I usually get this question, "Mel, what if I want to buy a house or need to save for something else important?" The answer is that big purchases and other large cash outlays need to be integrated into the allocation in Step 3.

I'm dogmatic about the first two steps, but not as much as in Step 3. I know people are going to want to do things like buy a home or plan a wedding or have a child. Life happens! So, in this step, you can slow down your investing temporarily and allocate those funds toward saving for large purchases and things that *really* matter.

You need the flexibility in this step because if you don't enjoy the journey *to* financial freedom, you won't enjoy it *in* financial freedom. Just remember that it slows down the building of your wealth, so you must be discerning and deliberate with when and how you do it.

It's also important to make a plan. For instance, if you know that you will need $12,000 in two years, then you allocate $500 per month for the next 24 months to fund that specific life goal. I would have the money automatically transferred to a high-yield savings account so you earn some income but it is safe and fully liquid.

Step 4: Pay Down Your Property

At this point, you can start to pay additional amounts to accelerate the paydown of the mortgage on your home. Now this is when I hear people say, "But, Mel, what about the tax deduction?" The tax deduction pales in comparison to the kind of returns you can get on investing the additional amounts.

There are nuances to consider when it comes to your personal circumstances and the current environment. For instance, it is more important to simply *have* the capacity to pay off your mortgage rather than *actually* paying it off. Those with very low interest rates on their home may choose to prioritize other investments rather than paying down a low-interest mortgage.

Step 5: Fund Your Kids' College

This one may land hard, but hear me out: This step is optional in my mind. My belief is that your priority needs to be your financial certainty before your kids' college funding. Your financial future is coming no matter what, so you need to make sure you are taken care of first. You have no good options if you don't have a fully funded future. Think about it—if you run out of money, you end up on government assistance, on your kids' couch, or a combination of both—none of which is a good option in my book.

Your kids, on the other hand, might not even go to college. They also have a number of options to offset costs, like going to community college and receiving grants or scholarships. Your kids have more options if you get them involved in college planning early, whereas when you get to your later years, you don't have options. Fund the certainty of your retirement before you fund the uncertainty of their college.

If you are the one preparing to go to college, keep in mind that you have more options than just student loans. Consider applying for scholarships, grants, and work-study programs to help offset the cost of tuition. You can also work while attending school. Consider whether the more expensive school is the way to go or if you can still get the same education and experiences needed for your success at a state school, or by starting at a community college and then transferring later. Remember, the decisions you make today can have a significant impact on your financial future.

I don't like using student loans to pay for college because too many students are buried in debt when they graduate and have no promise of being debt-free for decades. If you do take out a student loan, a good rule of thumb is to borrow no more than 12 to 18 months' worth of your expected salary after graduation. You'll need to research expected salaries in your field to prepare. This will allow you to pay off your debt quickly and start building wealth for your future.

PHASE 3, STEP 6: ENJOY YOUR AFFLUENCE

This is the place where your Affluence Vision is fully funded and you are living generously. You've created a Money Machine that allows you to do the things you want, how you want, and with whom you want. It's about impact, contribution, and generational change. This is where you can be fully behind the causes and movements that matter to you without regard to how you're going to make it financially, because the money side of your equation is taken care of.

* * *

So when you put all of this together in the Wealth Priority Ladder it will look like this:

THE WEALTH PRIORITY LADDER ™

AFFLUENCE — Living out your AFFLUENCE VISION, give generously & have legacy wealth — 6

COLLEGE — Fund education accounts, 529s, custodial Roths (ALL optional) — 5

PROPERTY — Accelerate payments on mortgage — 4

FREEDOM — 20%-25% of income to investing — 3

PEACE — 9-18 months peace of mind fund — 2B

CONSUMER — Eliminate destructive debt — 2A

COMFORT — $1500 or one months expenses — 1

Alternatives
Real Estate
Brokerage
Mega Backdoor
Backdoor Roth
HSA
401k Max
Roth IRA (maybe)
ESPP
401k Match

This is the path to build your Money Machine. It's where you will find your financial freedom, and it's the recipe for what to do with each dollar that comes in and what to prioritize in what order.

One of my mentors told me, "You should never leave sight of a goal without scheduling it." So take the time to jot down the answers to the following questions:

1. Based on my plan, when do I think I'll get through Phase 1?

2. When will I get through Phase 2?

3. When will I reach Phase 3? What date will I reevaluate my finances to set goals for Phases 4, 5, and 6?

These are not rhetorical questions. These are Action Items that you should be taking and putting on your calendar, because without scheduling your plan, it won't become a reality. So take 15 minutes to figure this out. You'll find useful tools to help you do this at MoneyMachineResources.com.

REMOVE THE FRICTION (MAKE IT EASY)

One of the biggest obstacles to systematic wealth building is that it's cumbersome and not easy—unless you automate it. If every time you need to make an investment or a transfer you physically have to call, write a check, or jump online to do it, it adds friction, which gets in the way of doing it consistently over a long period of time.

Credit card companies figured this out regarding your buying decisions. Yes, the idea of a credit card is to facilitate a "buy now, pay later" scenario, but the other thing it did was remove the friction from your buying decisions. It's effectively a decoupling of your money and your buying decision that allows you to make the decision easily and without much effort.

Think about this: If every time you needed to make a purchase, you had to count out cash, how many purchases do you think you would complete?

Heck, in today's world you don't even need to swipe a credit card. All you need to do is tap or bump your phone. No friction means more purchases.

What you should really be doing is putting *more* friction in your buying decisions and removing as much friction as possible from your investing decisions.

I remember working with a young couple a while back who liked their retail therapy. There were days where there were so many Amazon boxes arriving, they literally could not get to their front door. Maybe you can relate. I know at my house, it can get that way at times. In this case, it was clearly too easy for them to buy stuff. Here's what I had them do:

First, they removed every saved credit card number from their most frequented sites. This meant they had to get up and go get the card to input the number each time they wanted to buy something. Then I had them take all but one credit card and put them in a coffee can full of water, and then put the can in the freezer. If they wanted to buy something, they needed to get it and let it defrost before they could use one of the cards. I told them if they still wanted the thing that badly after it defrosted, go right ahead and buy.

I know it was extreme, but hey, it worked.

Friction is your friend when it comes to spending less money, but not when it comes to investing money or building wealth. The way you remove the friction from saving and investing is to set everything up on autopilot. I recommend automating as much as possible, including paying your bills. Everything is taken care of in the background with little, if any, effort on your part. This removes temptations from the process so you don't keep renegotiating with yourself to adjust the process and deviate from your plan.

The key is to talk to your banks and brokerage account holders to set up all transfers for savings and investing on an automatic basis. This means that on a certain day of the month, money will automatically get moved from your operating account to your investment accounts. Then the amount in the investment accounts will automatically be invested based on your standing instructions. Once this is set up, you can sit back and just focus on increasing your income, managing your expenses, and continuing to grow your money at an ever-accelerating rate.

Another benefit of automation is that it removes buying temptations. Removing temptations is an important step.

My wife, Stefanie, loves to cook and bake, and she has this cake display platter to showcase her work. It's kind of like the ones you might see in a bakery. The problem is, it has a clear glass cover on it. Okay, the clear cover isn't the problem . . . the fact that every time I walk by it, I see the goodies on the platter is the problem!

Now, even though she cooks and bakes healthy foods without sugars, grains, or dairy, there's still a limit to how much I should be eating. My problem is that every time I walk by the platter, I see the goodies, and I swear it's as if they're calling out my name. "Hey, Mel, one more won't hurt!" So what do I do? I grab one.

Then I walk by again, see the goodies in this clear display again, and (trust me . . .) hear the voices again . . . so I have another. Then another. Then another. By the end of the day, I'll have ended up eating like a dozen cookies, one cookie at a time. *Oops.* Temptation is not my friend.

You may not have a cake display tempting you, but you have social media and other influences in your life attempting to seduce you into putting your money toward things that don't align with the goals you've set for your life. Remember what you learned about in Chapter 10 so you can't be unconsciously triggered, and lean on your Belief Community for support.

Now that you have the recipe to build your Money Machine, it's time to understand the parts that make it up. Remember, the objective is to get your money to work harder for you than you did for it. In order to do that, we have to remove you as much as possible from the equation of the earning. This is where the Five Incomes™ come into play.

CHAPTER 13

THE FIVE INCOMES: A JOURNEY TO RECLAIM YOUR TIME

Disconnect your efforts from your results.

— MEL ABRAHAM

I no longer believe that having multiple streams of income is a luxury. It is an absolute requirement, especially for financial security and freedom.

I also don't believe—contrary to popular sentiment—that passive income is the answer.

True wealth requires engagement and involvement in your income streams. I know that many use the term *passive income*, but I don't like using that because it denotes a "set it and forget it" attitude. The fact is, you have a relationship with your money and wealth, and if you have a relationship with money (and you do in my book), then being passive or having a "set it and forget it" attitude is the end of the relationship. Instead, I use the term *leveraged*, because when you build a Money Machine, it leverages your active efforts around your money. You'll maximize the income you generate while minimizing the time you spend on it, but you should never become passive around it. It's about your relationship with the efforts and inputs, and with the money you make. Your goal is to make more money with less effort.

Given this, the following framework will explore the five different income types you can create and how they relate to building a Money Machine as well as leveraging your time and effort. It is this framework that allowed me to navigate cancer financially without having to drain savings or change our lifestyle.

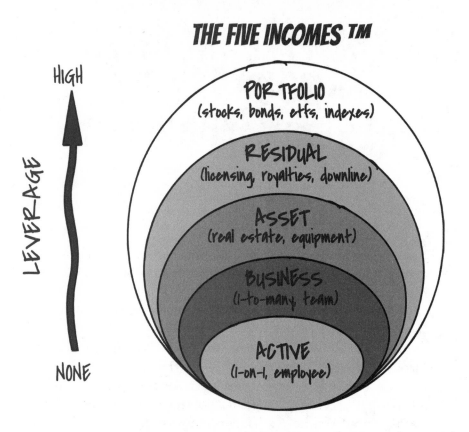

THE FIVE INCOMES ™

1. **Active Income.** The starting point for most people, active income is the direct exchange of your time and effort for money. This is the classic "hours for dollars" situation where you only make money when you're actively working. This could be as an employee, a solopreneur, running side hustles, or anything where the relationship between your time and effort is directly tied to the compensation you get. While

this may be necessary initially, it is not sustainable or scalable in the long term if you want your income to be independent of your time and effort.

2. **Business Income.** Moving from a one-on-one scenario to a one-to-many, business income allows you to serve a larger audience and scale your efforts with a team. This level of income provides you with more leverage and begins to free up your time. At this stage, the income is less directly dependent on you and more dependent on processes and the team. You as the figurehead and leader are still very involved, but less than you are at the active level.

   Now we move up to the categories that are the real building blocks of your Money Machine. This is because they remove you from the equation at a higher level.

3. **Asset-Based Income.** As we transition further into the realm of leveraged income, asset-based income involves acquiring assets like real estate, equipment, or hard assets. ("Hard" relates to physical or tangible assets that we can see, touch, and feel as opposed to intangible assets like intellectual property.) These assets generate rent or fees, allowing you to earn money without a one-to-one relationship between your time and efforts and earnings. Although you still need to be involved, your time investment is significantly less. Think about owning a couple of properties that are fully rented with tenants; the time you need to manage them is far less than in the lower categories of the Five Incomes Framework.

   For instance, I have one property where the tenant has been there since 1996. Not only that, he calls me when I don't cash his rent check fast enough. When there is anything to be done, he will volunteer to donate the labor if I pay for the materials. That's one good tenant.

4. **Residual Income.** This type of income often stems
   from intellectual property such as royalties from books,
   licensing deals, or white-labeling. (White labeling
   is allowing others to put their name on a product,
   service, or system you have for a fee.) It can also come
   from payouts associated with downlines from network
   marketing or direct-selling companies. The idea behind
   residual income is that you invest time up front to create
   something of value, and you continue to get paid for its
   use long after you've created it.

   Let's take my courses and books, for example.
   I created them by investing a bunch of time and
   effort into them. I then set up a mechanism to have
   the selling and delivery on autopilot and continue
   to collect royalties or fees from something that I
   created previously with little or no continuing effort
   on my part.

5. **Portfolio Income.** The highest level of leveraged
   income involves investing in paper assets like stocks,
   bonds, ETFs, index funds, mutual funds, real estate
   investment trusts, annuities, and trust deed lending.
   Although you still need to be involved in managing
   your investments, the time commitment is minimal
   compared to the potential earnings. You can hold
   these assets or investments outright or in retirement
   plans, but by and large, they are securities that can
   appreciate or pay cash flows over time. They all have
   differing levels of risk involved, and any investments
   should be part of a detailed financial plan that is
   driven by your Affluence Vision.

   As this part of your Money Machine reaches
   a critical mass, you will likely have a team of
   advisors to watch over it and make sure that you're
   in the appropriate types of investment for your
   circumstance, your risk tolerance, and your capacity.

During the beginning stages of your financial journey, most if not all of your income will come from the Active Income category of the Five Incomes. There's nothing wrong with this as long as you're also building other income streams that don't require a direct relationship between your time and effort and the income generated. Your Money Machine is built from assets accumulated in the top three levels of income—Asset, Residual, and Portfolio. The goal is to have enough income from these levels to cover a minimum of 80 percent of your lifestyle needs. This is how I was able to navigate cancer financially without having to drain assets, change our lifestyle, or sell things. Here's what happened.

At the time I was diagnosed with cancer, 100 percent of our lifestyle was paid for with income from the Active Income and Business Income levels. Although we were generating income from the other three levels, we weren't using it to live, simply using it to grow the Money Machine even bigger.

After the diagnosis, I decided I needed to totally focus on beating the cancer and shut my businesses down to almost nothing. At the same time, I told my wealth team to flip the switch on the Money Machine and have it pay us enough of the income to continue our lifestyle during this time.

More specifically, our Money Machine is built with ETFs, index funds, and dividend- or interest-paying investments. These investments, aside from appreciation in value, also generate monthly cash flows. Before my diagnosis, we were reinvesting all the income from the investments to continue to grow the machine. (This is the effect of compounding and how your money gets to a critical mass so it works harder for you than you did for it.) After my diagnosis, I simply had my team take a portion of the income and send it to us to pay our living costs. This happened without us having to sell or liquidate the investments or drain any savings.

This meant I no longer had to put any time or effort into generating income. That is the beauty of building an effective Money Machine. This is exactly what I want for you and what this whole book is about.

So, in the context of the Five Incomes, it looked a bit like this:

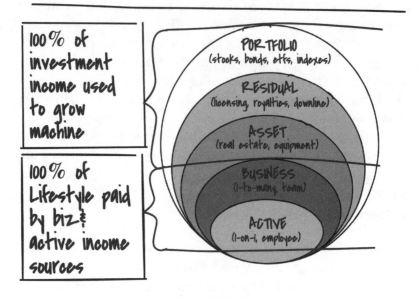

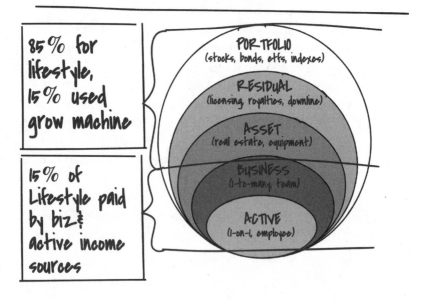

You will see that the majority of our lifestyle after diagnosis came from the income we were generating from the top three asset classes. Then once I got beyond the cancer, we flipped it back to the way it was before I was diagnosed.

The nice thing is, the Money Machine still continued to grow even though we were using some of the income. And once I came through the cancer and felt I wanted to get back at it again, I reversed the process. I told the team to shut the machine off and restarted my income from my Active Income and Business Income pursuits.

The beautiful thing about achieving financial freedom is that you get to live a life by design and choice rather than by survival. By following a proven process like this, one step at a time, you can have the same thing.

The core of building your Money Machine is built on the Wealth Priority Ladder and the Five Incomes, but there are some things you can do to elevate the income you make by getting paid more and being seen as a higher value in the market or company you are serving. Imagine if you could get the market or your company to see you as 20 percent more valuable, resulting in your getting paid 20 percent more—in most cases for the same level of effort. It's a good place to start. Remember, more money will lead to an acceleration to your financial freedom number simply because you have more money to work with.

Grow

Asset planning leads to income flowing.

— MEL ABRAHAM

CHAPTER 14

GROWING YOUR MONEY MACHINE

Your direction is more important than your speed.

— MEL ABRAHAM

Remember the Wealth Creation Curve from Part I? This is where we start to navigate the curve and eat up the Wealth Flatline. Why does this curve even happen?

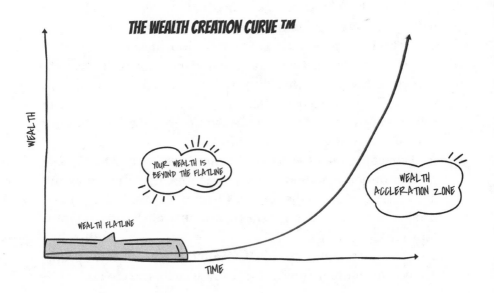

THE WEALTH CREATION CURVE ™

The acceleration comes from a few key things that converge over time. The first is your consistent application of the principles and diligent investing over the long term. Even though you don't see huge results in the beginning, you understand that your behaviors and small steps matter. Then there is the math behind the curve. Over time, your money gains velocity and momentum as a result of something we call *compounding*.

Remember those employees (dollars) you gave a job description to? Here's where it matters. Because after a while, those dollars make more money for you than you ever put in. Here's how it works:

Invest $1,000 at a 10 percent annual return, and at the end of the year, you'll have $1,100. But that $100 you earned now starts to earn money too. So in year two, the $1,100 earns another 10 percent, which turns into $1,210. Effectively, the dollars earned begin to earn on themselves. If we take this out 10 years, this $1,000 will become $2,594—and that's without you adding any more to that initial investment and simply staying in the game . . . on the Wealth Creation Curve. What happens in another 10 years? It becomes $6,728.

Think about this: At this point, a 10 percent annual return has you earning your entire initial $1,000 investment again every year. This is money velocity and momentum at work.

Many people mistakenly believe that building wealth requires large investments or that only those with a lot of assets can achieve financial freedom. Hopefully, you see that the power of compounding and time can be the most powerful element in your arsenal to building your Money Machine.

Remember that *The National Study of Millionaires* found that 79 percent of the millionaires surveyed were first-generation millionaires.[1] This means they didn't inherit their wealth. They didn't win it. They created it from scratch. And they did it based on these principles.

More important, it means that if almost eight out of ten people can become millionaires starting from scratch, then so can you!

UNLOCKING THE POWER OF COMPOUNDING AND THE RULE OF 72

If you want to get a ballpark of what your money could grow into, you can apply something called the Rule of 72. This is a simple formula that helps you estimate how long it will take for your investment to double in value, given a fixed annual rate of return. To use the Rule of 72, simply divide 72 by the annual interest rate (expressed as a percentage). The result is the number of years it will take for your investment to double.

For example, if you have an investment with an 8 percent annual return, it would take approximately 9 years for your investment to double (72 ÷ 8 = 9). This rule is a powerful tool for understanding the potential growth of your investments and the importance of consistent, long-term investing.

Now that you understand the power of compounding and the Rule of 72, how should you apply it to building your wealth and Money Machine?

Here are some practical steps you can take to apply these principles and build your wealth over time:

1. **Start early.** The sooner you begin investing, the more time your investments have to compound and grow. Even if you can only afford to invest a small amount initially, getting started is crucial. Remember, you want to get past the Wealth Flatline because everything after that grows at an accelerated pace.

2. **Invest consistently.** Investing regularly into your accounts, even if in smaller amounts to start, can lead to substantial growth over time. Remember to remove the friction by automating this part like we talked about in the previous chapter.

3. **Choose investments with a long-term view.** Your investing and building a Money Machine isn't just about today. In fact, it's more about your tomorrows being as fruitful as possible. With that said, make

sure you're considering a long-term view with your investing. I get that the market and economy will go up and go down in the short term, but over the long term it typically goes up. In fact, the stock market is up on average usually eight out of ten years, or 80 percent of the time. We'll go a bit deeper on the types of investments to think about in a bit.

4. **Reinvest your earnings.** Instead of withdrawing your investment earnings, reinvest them to take full advantage of compounding. This is where your money velocity and momentum will come from.

5. **Be patient.** Compounding takes time to work its magic. Be patient and avoid the temptation to withdraw your investments early or make impulsive decisions based on short-term market fluctuations.

The principles of compounding and the Rule of 72 demonstrate that even small sums can lead to big wins when it comes to investing.

The key to money velocity and momentum is to focus on consistency rather than perfection. By taking small, consistent steps toward financial goals, you can build momentum and make progress over time. This will help you achieve greater financial security, freedom, and peace of mind.

CHAPTER 15

SAVINGS VS. GAMBLING VS. TRADING VS. INVESTING

The stock market can either be used as a casino to gamble in or a place where your wealth is built.

— MEL ABRAHAM

Before we get to the types of investments you can use to build your Money Machine, let's clarify the differences between savings, gambling, trading, and investing.

SAVINGS

Savings and investing will be the two primary ways of managing your money.

Savings is best for parking money in an account to be used for some purpose in the short term or until the right investment opportunity comes up. It can be at a bank, a credit union, an online bank, or even a brokerage house. The key is that it is accessible to you and not going to go up and down with the stock market. Effectively, if you put $100 in, you can get $100 out plus a bit of interest you may have earned.

There are a couple of account types you might see for this:

- **Traditional savings account.** This is the most basic type of savings account offered by banks and credit unions. Traditional savings accounts generally offer a low interest rate (okay, barely anything), easy access to your funds, and a high level of safety since they're insured by the Federal Deposit Insurance Corporation (FDIC) or the National Credit Union Administration (NCUA) up to certain limits.

- **High-yield savings account.** HYSAs are similar to traditional savings accounts but offer higher interest rates. These accounts are designed to help your money grow at a faster pace. They're also FDIC- or NCUA-insured, and you can access your money relatively easily. Many of these are at online banks with a lower expense structure, which allows them to offer much higher savings rates than traditional banks without necessitating that the funds be locked into a specific term. My criteria for a high-yield cash account are that it *must* be fully liquid (the money can be accessed anytime), it *must* be fully insured (some online banks actually have insurance beyond the current FDIC and NCUA $250,000 limit because of the network they are in), and there can be *no* fees—not a dime for them to have your money.

  I use these accounts extensively to park my short-term cash and make at least more than I would in a traditional savings account. This is where I have my Peace of Mind Fund, my tax accounts, and any other short-term cash needs—short term being five years or less. I will also park money there temporarily until I find a specific investment I want to invest in so it is earning while waiting. In fact, if you're unsure where to invest, just put any money you have into an HYSA so that you're exercising the muscle of savings, and then we can get to investing it later.

- **Money market account.** A money market account combines features of both savings and checking accounts. These accounts typically offer higher interest rates than traditional savings accounts and may come with limited check-writing privileges or a debit card. Money market accounts are also insured by the FDIC or NCUA, but they often require a higher minimum balance to avoid fees.

- **Certificate of deposit.** A CD is a time-deposit account that requires you to commit your funds for a specified term, usually ranging from a few months to several years. In exchange for locking up your money, you receive a higher interest rate than what's typically offered on traditional savings accounts. CDs are also FDIC- or NCUA-insured, but withdrawing your funds before the term ends can result in early-withdrawal penalties.

When choosing the right type of savings account, consider factors such as interest rates, accessibility, fees, minimum balance requirements, and your financial goals. By comparing the different types of accounts available, you can find the best option for your individual needs and maximize the growth of your savings.

GAMBLING

Now let's go to the other extreme: gambling. This discussion will be short.

Gambling is just that—you're playing games of chance or speculation. Sometimes you win; more often you lose. There are no assurances, and typically there is no strategy. Oh, I know the person that's selling you into the gambit will tell you there's strategy, but there typically isn't anything of substance there. Often there's no business model behind it, no possible growth, and not much in the way of operations. These schemes can show up disguised as investments, investing memes, or even a recommendation from a friend. There's always one big rule in gambling: gamble only what you're willing to lose, or don't do it at all.

Let me give you a tangible example of how this can show up disguised as an investment. Let's talk about GameStop. For all intents and purposes, this company is in decline and at risk of shutting down. But on a whim, a group of investors driven by a meme on a subreddit called r/WallStreetBets started talking about it and showing that they were buying it. ("Subreddits" are what the communities on the website Reddit are called.) More people jumped in to buy the stock. While the buying was happening, it started to drive the price of the stock up.

In April 2020, the stock price was at $2.57 per share. At its peak on January 28, 2021, the stock price hit $483 per share. Yep, you read that right: $483. Did the company change? No! Did it have new possibilities for growth? No! Did people make money? Yep! Did people lose money? Oh, *huge*! The only thing that really drove the price increase was the talk on Reddit that generated the buying, but when the dust settled, it all came crashing down again to the reality of the fact that GameStop was in decline and struggling to survive.

All I can say is, don't fall prey to these types of things, or it could cost you big-time. No matter how much FOMO (fear of missing out) you have or how good it sounds, let others play that game. Instead, you play the long game of building a sustainable Money Machine.

TRADING

Are trading and investing the same thing?

In a word, *no!*

Trading is a job. It is you sitting in front of a computer day by day, minute by minute, watching the stock market and trying to buy and sell in moments or days to make some money. It isn't driven by long-term vision and building a Money Machine as we are doing here. It can be a high-stress, high-adrenaline type of lifestyle. It isn't leveraged like we talked about in the Five Incomes. Can you make money trading? Yes, and I have. But I also don't trade a lot because I can't and don't want to be in a high-stress situation or sitting in front of my computer all the time. But most important, because I built a Money Machine, I don't need to.

Warren Buffett said something to the effect of, "Calling yourself an investor when all you're doing is trading is like calling yourself a romantic when all you're doing is one-night stands." Oooh . . . good ol' Warren.

The chart below may give you a deeper perspective around the difference between trading and investing. Like I said, I do both, but I understand what I'm doing and the differences.

TRADING VS. INVESTING

TRADING		INVESTING
BUY & SELL BASED ON PRICE MOVEMENTS	WHAT IS IT?	BUY & HOLD BASED ON STOCK VALUE
SHORT TERM, QUICK ENTRY & EXIT	TIMELINE	LONG TERM, EXIT DISTANT FROM ENTRY
ALL SHORT TERM, ORDINARY TAX RATES	CAPITAL GAINS	MOSTLY LONG TERM, LONG TERM RATES
RISK HIGH DUE TO SPEED & SHORT TERM	RISKINESS	RISK LOW DUE TO LONG TERM
ONLY STOCKS & OPTIONS, QUICK ENTRY/EXIT	SECURITIES	STOCKS, BONDS, ETFS, MUTUALS & NOTES
ONGOING PROFITS FROM ENTRY & EXITS	INTENTION	CAPITAL APPRECIATION & REINVESTMENT
TECHNICAL ANALYSIS, MOVING AVG & CHARTS	TOOLS	FUNDAMENTAL ANALYSIS, EPS & RATIOS
BUY LOW/SELL HIGH, SELL SHORT/BUY LOW	STRATEGY	BUY AND HOLD FOR COMPANY GROWTH
STOP LOSSES SET BEFORE TRADE OPEN	PROTECTION	PRIMARILY HOLDING THROUGH VOLATILITY
FREQUENT TRANSACTIONS, FREQUENT CHARGES	COSTS	LIMITED TRANSACTIONS, LIMITED FEES

INVESTING

Okay, now let's take a look at investing, investments, and what is available to you. This is where I want you to build your Money Machine. This is where you will create a sustainable wealth machine that can support your Affluence Vision and lifestyle without you being constantly involved on a daily basis. This is the long-term game built on discipline, patience, consistency, and the principles we've talked about through the Affluence Cash Flow Matrix,

Wealth Priority Ladder, Wealth Creation Curve, and Five Incomes. When these converge, you will see the power behind it all.

Investing is all about putting your money into different assets that will go up in value and/or generate cash flows consistently over the long term. The types of assets include things like stocks, bonds, mutual funds, real estate, or commodities and various alternative investments.

Investing involves taking on some level of risk, as there is no guarantee that your investment will increase in value, and you could potentially lose some or all of your investment. In fact, the higher your possible return from an investment, the higher risk you usually take on. This is why diversification is so important. *Diversification* simply means to have multiple types of stocks and investments, so if one goes bad you don't lose everything.

You can never make an investing decision without considering the risk of the investment. We will talk deeper about risk in a bit, but know it is something that everyone needs to consider. It's different for everyone based on circumstances, age, risk tolerance, and capacity. This is why there's no one-size-fits-all approach to investing and wealth building.

The graph here gives you a picture of how risk and return are connected:

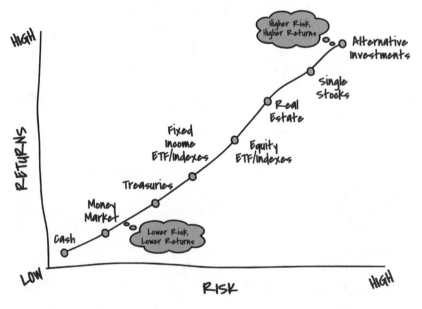

With this as the backdrop, let's take a walk down investment lane so you can get a perspective of the investment options that you have access to. Then I'll tell you what I would focus on first as you build.

Bonds

Bonds are a type of investment that involves lending money to a company or government in exchange for interest payments over time. Bonds are generally less risky than stocks, but they also offer lower returns.

Stocks

Stocks are ownership shares in a company. When you buy a stock, you become a part owner of the company that issues it and can profit from its growth and success. As the company grows, the stock price can rise. Also, some companies pay a portion of their profits to shareholders in the form of dividends. However, stocks can be volatile and carry risk. Investing in individual stocks requires research and knowledge of a company and its industry.

When you're starting out, I don't recommend investing in individual stocks like this, because you're too exposed to the volatility. If a single stock happens to be your primary or only holding, you can be destroyed if it declines.

Let's take this as an example: Imagine if your primary or only holding was this stock in the following graph, which dropped from over $200 per share to less than $20—losing over 90 percent of its value. In fact, I saw someone post in a forum that he had invested over $200,000 in it and lost over 50 percent of that in the decline. He was asking what he should do at that point. But here's the problem . . . he then said this was all he had. *Ugh.* He had wiped out half of his wealth because he was in a single stock versus diversified. Even worse, this company never recovered and was taken over, but the shareholders were effectively wiped out. So he likely lost it all unless he got out before the closing of the doors.

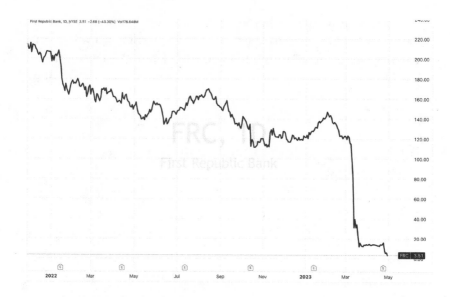

Full disclosure: I do invest in individual stocks. But it isn't where I started. I did it after I had critical mass in my portfolio so I didn't take on too much risk. You reduce this risk by using mutual funds, ETFs, or index funds, which we're going to discuss next.

Mutual Funds

When you invest in a mutual fund, you actually invest in a basket of stocks instead of just a single stock. This gives you more diversification and reduces—but doesn't eliminate—your risks. It also allows you access to a bunch of stocks at one time for one price versus you trying to build your own diversified basket of stocks.

The one thing to be aware of with these funds is that they're each actively managed by a fund manager. This means that they carry more fees and expenses, which could reduce your returns. Last, some studies have shown that over the long term, actively managed funds don't outperform the stock market itself. This is what gave rise to index funds and ETF funds, which we'll talk about next.

Exchange-Traded Funds (ETFs) and Index Funds

ETFs are similar to mutual funds, but they trade like stocks on an exchange. They typically have much lower fees and give you the diversification that you should have. An index fund is similar to an ETF but can be a bit higher in fees, and it trades only at the end of the day—not throughout the day like an ETF.

Both ETFs and index funds track indexes like the S&P 500. By *tracking*, I mean that the portfolio and holdings of the fund are built to mimic various indexes. For example, an index fund tracking the Dow Jones Industrial Average would invest in the same 30 large and publicly owned companies that compose that index. There are many different indexes that can be tracked.

Here's the simplest way to think about an index. Imagine you're in a candy store, and there are hundreds of different candies to choose from. There are chocolates, gummies, lollipops, and many more. To help you find the candies you like, the store has a big sign called the "Candy Index."

The Candy Index is a list that shows you all the different candies and how popular they are with other kids. The most popular candy is at the top of the list, and the least popular is at the bottom. Just like a candy store, the stock market has many different choices of companies, and an index is a list that shows you how well these companies are doing compared to each other.

By looking at the Candy Index, you can easily see which candies are the most loved, and it helps you decide which candies you might want to try. In the same way, a stock market index helps people see which companies are doing well, so they can make smart choices with their money.

How does this idea relate to an index fund or an ETF? They are like a giant candy bag that already has a small piece of each candy in the store. By getting a bag, you're making sure you get to taste all the different candies without having to pick them one by one. This way, if one candy turns out to be not as sweet as you had hoped, it's okay because you still have lots of other candies to enjoy. And the best part is, as the candies become more popular, your candy bag becomes more valuable too! That's what ETFs and index funds do with the stock market, giving you a piece of many different companies to help your money grow.

Mutual funds, index funds, and ETFs are all built to allow an investor to invest into a basket of stocks at an affordable cost instead of trying to buy a bunch of individual stocks, which would also require more money. This is because when you invest in the fund and it gets a bunch of investors' money, then the fund buys the stocks. This way, all the investors in the fund are sharing in the cost of the stocks.

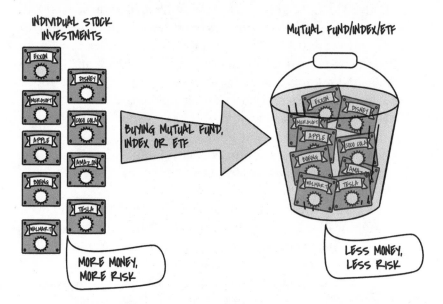

The most popular index funds track the S&P 500. But several other indexes are widely used as well, including:

- Wilshire 5000 Total Market Index, the largest U.S. equities index

- MSCI EAFE Index, consisting of foreign stocks from Europe, Australasia, and the Far East

- Bloomberg U.S. Aggregate Bond Index, which follows the total bond market

- NASDAQ Composite Index, made up of 3,000 stocks listed on the NASDAQ exchange

- Dow Jones Industrial Average (DJIA), consisting of 30 large-cap companies

I love using ETFs in my portfolio to get access to market returns and diversification without taking on high fees or expenses. It's a great way to make an investment in a diversified basket as if you invested directly in an index.

Target-Date Index Funds

Target-date funds are like ETFs and index funds, but they build their holdings based on a date in the future to maximize your returns by that time. Usually, the date is based on when you want or need the money: the fund manager adjusts the portfolio to be less risky as you get closer to when you'd need it.

For example, if you expect to retire in 2055, you simply pick a 2055 fund. The holdings are more aggressive early on and then get adjusted to be less aggressive as you approach 2055. This allows you to maximize your growth in the early years while minimizing your risk in the later years without your having to make those decisions directly. The automatic adjustments that get made as the target date approaches is what they call the *glide path* of the fund.

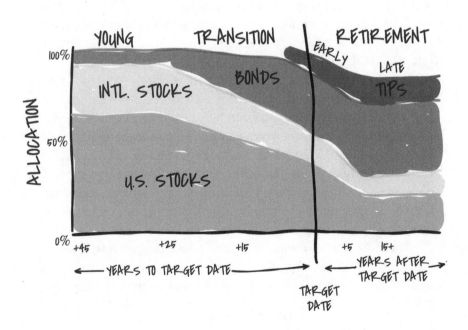

I honestly like these funds, especially for when you're just starting out, because they reduce complexity and decision friction, and they get you in the game. You'll be in an investment that you know is geared toward your timeline and needs. Once you get critical mass to your portfolio and have more to work with, you may shift to picking and choosing specific funds, but this avoids most of that. Pretty much all you have to know is the date you want to work with, and you can choose the funds that work for you.

This is where I most often have people start investing.

Real Estate

Real estate investing involves buying and holding property for rental income or capital appreciation. It can also be more speculative, with flipping properties that you buy and fix up. I love real estate as a long-term investment, but there are some things to consider. Properties often require a fair amount of money to get into them and require you to take on debt. They come with a lot of transaction costs in the form of commissions, fees, and closing costs. They typically take longer to buy or sell, which makes them less liquid compared to other investments.

I don't often recommend starting with this type of investment because of these reasons, but also for three other reasons. We just said that it takes more money to get into and isn't as easy to get out of. You also can't diversify. At most, you are buying one property at a time. At the beginning of your wealth journey, this complexity plus the lack of diversification can be issues if you aren't careful.

Imagine you invest in a property and it sits vacant for a while—or worse, you have a tenant who stops paying rent and you can't get them out without going through a lengthy legal eviction process. Now, not only is your money tied up in an asset that isn't making you money like you thought it would, it's costing you money because you need to keep the mortgage and real estate taxes current.

The third reason I don't recommend starting with this investment is the possible impact on your lifestyle. If you don't want to be a landlord and deal with landlord issues like repairs, vacancies, evictions, and the like, don't get into real estate directly.

The key behind any real estate investment is to always remember that the money in real estate is made on the purchase, not the sale. You need to buy it right, in the right way, at the right price.

Alternative Investments

Alternative investments can include assets such as commodities, hedge funds, private equity, precious metals, or art. They are generally considered riskier and less liquid than traditional investments, and you really need specialized knowledge to invest in them effectively. I don't recommend these for those starting out, but they may be an option, once you reach a critical mass with your portfolio, to bring other types of investments in. But if you do, it has to be for a very strategic and specific reason, so that they accomplish what you intend for them to accomplish. Otherwise, you're just collecting investments with no plan or strategy.

* * *

Always realize that no matter what the investment is, it involves some level of risk. That means you could lose some or all the money you invested. This is why it's important to work from a financial plan and to make sure you have a clear understanding of the level of risk you *can* tolerate as well as the level of risk you *should* tolerate. Once you understand all this, it's easier to make appropriate investing decisions that work for you.

WHERE TO BEGIN?

Now you might be wondering, *Where do I even begin?* If you're new to investing, you can start by looking into a discount broker. Vanguard, Schwab, and Fidelity are the major United States brokers. Start by opening an account and fund it with the amount that you want to invest.

Here's a crucial point to remember: funding the account is not the same as buying investments through the account. A lot of people say, "Well, I've invested in my IRA," but when I look at their account, all they did was *fund* the IRA. They put $6,500 in there but didn't tell the IRA where to invest, so it's not working for them. You still have to direct your dollars where to go so they can do their jobs and produce more money for you.

Investing money in an investment account is like sending a three-stage rocket into financial orbit. The first stage is selecting the ideal launch pad (type of account) based on your mission's needs, such as a traditional launch pad (pretax), a futuristic launch pad (after tax), or a versatile lunar lander (IRA). The second stage is filling up the rocket's fuel tank (putting money into the account), which will propel it toward the stars. The final stage is igniting the engines (buying the investments) that will ultimately take your rocket (money) on a journey through the galaxy of financial growth, allowing it to soar toward your desired destination.

If you're ready to take your first step, just look for a target index fund and hit Buy. That's it. But as you advance through what these discount brokers offer, you can dive into the world of stocks, bonds, and mutual funds to build a portfolio that's tailored to your unique financial goals—and your risk tolerance, which is important to discuss more.

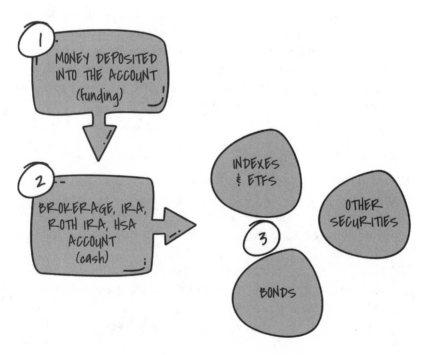

CHAPTER 16

RISK (CAN VS. SHOULD)

The ultimate risk is in trying to avoid all risks.
Your wealth will be on the other side of calculated risks.

— MEL ABRAHAM

You can't talk about investing without talking about the four-letter word . . . *risk.*

I get it, many people are risk averse. They tell me they don't want to risk their money. The problem is that you can't invest and not have any risk at all. If you do have no risk, then you're probably not investing at all. The real question is, how can you invest while taking on the appropriate amount of risk for you and your situation?

The path to financial success and wealth creation is paved with both opportunities and risks. As investors (because that's what you are now), it's our responsibility to navigate this landscape and make informed decisions that minimize the chances of loss. I will share my insights on avoiding risk in investing. By following these guidelines, you can build a robust investment portfolio designed to withstand market fluctuations.

THE RISK PROFILING TRIAD™

Risk is a delicate balance between three specific things. If you get it wrong, you could fall way short of your financial freedom number, or you could lose everything.

Surely we want to minimize risk, but we need to balance it with what we're trying to accomplish with our investment goals from a wealth-building standpoint. Also, everyone's risk profile is different. I can take a different level of risk than you can. You can take on a different level of risk at 20 years old than at 50 years old. Your risk changes and moves with your circumstances and situation.

What drives your level of risk are three specific factors that I call the Risk Profiling Triad™. You've probably heard the terms *risk tolerance* and *risk profile*, but what goes into them?

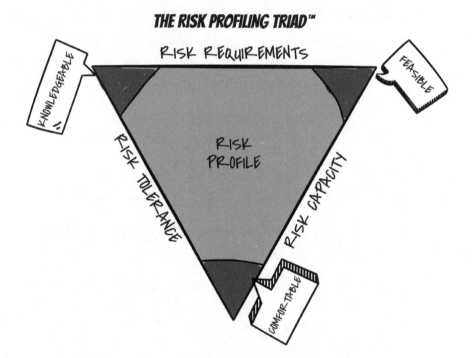

THE RISK PROFILING TRIAD™

Hopefully, this framework will help you better understand risk so you'll be better equipped as you build your Money Machine.

Its first factor is what I call *risk requirements*. We often don't think about them, but as we discussed earlier, an investment return is tied to the risk you are willing to take on. More return, more risk. Lower return, lower risk.

Risk requirements have you ask, "How much risk do I need to take on to accomplish the investment growth I need to hit my wealth numbers?" Here's what I mean: Say you have $500,000 but need to get to $1,000,000 in five years. You would need an average return of 14.9 percent to get there. But what happens if you had eight years to get there? Then the return you require would be only 9.1 percent. So your first task is to understand the requirements to get you to the target you're trying to achieve.

Now with this understanding, it doesn't mean you just go after investments to achieve that, because you need to look at the other two elements of your profile: *risk tolerance* and *risk capacity*.

Let's take a look at risk tolerance first. This comes down to your willingness to take on risk. Let's face it, there are some people who are adrenaline junkies, and others who are scared of their own shadow. Tolerance is more about the psychology and emotions around the level of risk you're willing to accept. It's like your pain tolerance. Everyone is different. I have a high pain tolerance. In fact, surgeons couldn't believe that I didn't feel the tumor in my bladder long before I had symptoms. It was larger than a baseball, and I was totally oblivious.

The other side of the coin is risk capacity. That's the amount of risk you can take on and recover from if things go against you. This can be impacted by things like your age, wealth, and income.

You can think of the three risk factors in this way:

- Risk requirements are how much you need to get in returns so you can hit your goals and target.

- Risk tolerance is how much risk you can take on without being uncomfortable—or, in other words, it's your willingness.

- Risk capacity is all about the limit of risk you can take and still be safe and on track.

Here's the other thing that comes from understanding the relationship between these three factors. When you know your requirements and your tolerance, you become knowledgeable of what you want and what you're willing to do. By knowing your tolerance and your capacity, you become comfortable with the investing decisions you're making. And when you're clear on your requirements and capacity, you can see how feasible your plan is, given the timeline you set forth.

ACTION ITEM — Take a risk assessment to get a better understanding of your level of tolerance.

ACTION ITEM — Review your financial plan and financial freedom number to clarify what your risk requirements are to achieve them.

ALLOCATION AND DIVERSIFICATION

Any discussion about risk would not be complete without talking about asset allocation and asset diversification. They are two related but different concepts that will impact your risk and the level of risk in your portfolio.

Asset allocation is deciding what types of assets (asset classes) you want to invest in. They could be things like ETFs, stock, real estate, bonds, and alternatives.

Once you decide on the allocation, then you can determine their diversification. Diversification is what specifically you will invest in inside each asset class. For instance, if you say you want 25 percent of your portfolio in ETFs, diversification answers the question of which ETFs and how much of each.

Here's how I think of the relationship between these two elements. Asset allocation is like deciding which type of car you want to buy. Maybe you want an SUV. Then diversification is about which make or model of SUV, and what the features you want are.

The chart below shows how it works in portfolio design.

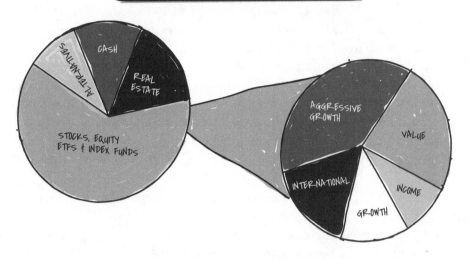

ASSET ALLOCATION VS DIVERSIFICATION

Although the above breakdown may look complicated, it isn't where you start. Everyone (including me) has to start slow and with a very simple structure. Then over time, as you reach critical mass in your investments, you can diversify more. For instance, most people start with a simple target-date fund because it takes care of the diversification for you. At the beginning, your portfolio may look more like this:

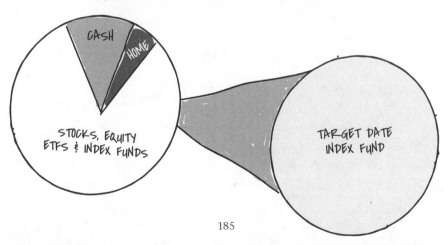

ASSET ALLOCATION VS DIVERSIFICATION

YOU NEED TO START SOMEWHERE - START SIMPLE

Most of the time, we start with one asset class beyond cash and possibly a home.

If I were starting today, I would take my cash and invest it with a target fund, and that's it. Then, as my portfolio grew to $300,000, I would diversify some of the index funds to be in more than one. Then I might get into real estate or other things down the road. But I would start simple in the beginning and continue to educate myself on where I can go from there as my portfolio grows. By taking this approach, you get to make fewer decisions, and there's less complexity. Fewer decisions and less complexity creates less friction to your investing, which gets you in the investing game and keeps you there. It also reduces risks of being in the wrong assets for your age and stage of life. Furthermore, it will be automatically adjusted to a portfolio that is appropriate for your age without you thinking about it.

We covered a lot of ground in this part, but this is the foundation to building your Money Machine and ultimately your financial freedom. Now is the time for you to get in there and start executing and building the behaviors, habits, and choices that bring the concepts in this part of the book to life in your world. These will be the actions that set you up for the ideal life you created with your Affluence Vision in Part II.

Protect

Protection is the final necessity of your affluence and legacy.

— Mel Abraham

CHAPTER 17

PROTECTING YOUR MONEY MACHINE

*Build a moat of protection around what
you earn and your ability to enjoy it.*

— MEL ABRAHAM

Now that you're creating assets, how do you protect them from loss?

There are risks all around us that can threaten our financial wealth, our well-being, and our ability to build wealth. This happens to be the reality of the world we live in today. Although it may not be fun to talk about the possible doom and gloom, I see part of my job as keeping you safe and equipping you to protect your assets, your ability to earn, and the legacy you are creating.

It's one thing to create wealth, but it's a whole other thing to keep it. I've already shared the stats that show that as much as 80 percent of millionaires are first-generation, but even more staggering is that, according to the Williams Group wealth consultancy, by the second generation, almost 70 percent of the wealth is gone. And by the next generation, over 90 percent is gone![1]

Risks can come from a whole host of places, including places you may not even have thought of. For example, I remember reading about the case of a teenager who was driving his grandma's car when he got in an accident. He went through a stop sign, but his view was somewhat blocked by the hedges on the corner. The person that he hit ended up suing the teenager's parents, the city for not requiring the hedges to be trimmed, the owner of the house where the hedges were, and the grandma. The surprising thing is, they were able to get a judgment against Grandma for $500,000, because it was her car.

The point is that risks are all around you, and they can bite if you aren't careful. The key is to understand the different exposures that may exist and do what you can to reduce or completely remove them from your world. Your desire should be to protect what you earn as well as your ability to earn.

Before we dive in, though, here's my disclaimer: All the information in this chapter is for your education only and not direct legal advice. You always want to seek competent legal advice to make sure you're protected effectively in your country and state.

With that out of the way, let's dive in and explore some ways to safeguard your wealth and ensure long-term financial stability.

THE DIRTY DOZEN DREAM KILLERS

When I work with my clients, we typically start with what I call the Dirty Dozen Dream Killers™. Let's walk through these quickly before I dig a little deeper into some specific risks I want you to be prepared for.

1. **Accident.** There can be exposure from accidents such as vehicle, slip and fall, equipment malfunction, or some other unintentional cause; hence the name *accident.* Just because something was an accident doesn't exempt you from some responsibility if it's deemed your fault. These risks are usually insurable with auto, premise, or liability insurance. The more successful you are, the higher your limits should be.

2. **Health and Disability.** This is a big one, especially given the cost of health care these days and the fact that your ability to earn depends on your health. One of the biggest causes of bankruptcy today is unpaid

medical bills. I get it: health insurance is expensive (and one of the most screwed-up industries around, but don't get me started). Still, it's a necessity to preserve your life, your lifestyle, and your wealth.

Your ability to earn becomes especially important if you haven't built enough leveraged income sources to support your lifestyle. If you get sick, injured, or disabled (temporarily or permanently), your earnings would be put into jeopardy, and with it your future. This is an insurable risk with a long-term disability insurance policy. According to the commissioners standard ordinary mortality table, at no time during the ages of 35 to 65 is the risk of death greater than the risk of disability.[2]

I've had a long-term disability insurance policy for decades now and have used it a few times. Remember my bike accident? Well, during my recovery, I was able to use that policy to pay me well over $100,000 so I could focus on my physical therapy and rehab without worrying if I could pay my bills. It totally took a ton of financial pressure off of me.

The reality is, although death is inevitable, disability is far more financially devastating if you aren't prepared for it. Although there are short-term disability insurance policies available, I don't usually recommend them. Your Peace of Mind Fund should be enough to carry you through any short-term emergencies of a few weeks.

3. **Family Members.** I know they're family, but sometimes they can be your biggest exposure. For instance, if you have minor children who drive, their getting into any type of accident beyond your insured limits puts you at risk. You may do nothing wrong, but a family member could, which could impact you.

4. **Divorce.** This is a big risk to you and your financial future. Now, I'm a believer in marriage and a hopeless romantic at heart, but I also think that we give up too easily in relationships and maybe rush into marriage before rationally considering it. Either way, divorce shouldn't be the solution—or at least not the first thing you think about when there's a bump in your road. Communication and learning to respect each other is, but I digress. This isn't a relationship book. But you should realize that a divorce can put all your planning and the building of your future at risk, and that isn't even counting the emotional costs with it.

5. **No Cushion.** Murphy's Law is real and can come home to roost if you're not prepared. The unexpected emergency, bill, or expense can do you in if you don't have a proper cushion set aside. This is why the Wealth Priority Ladder is so very important.

6. **Debt.** *Boom!* This is the big one. As a society, we carry far too much debt. Debt is the devil disguised in today's desires while robbing from your future. If you need to go into debt to buy something, it means you can't afford it in the first place. You need to eliminate the use of debt (at least consumer debt) from your life. Debt will destroy your business, eat your assets, and eliminate your future if things go wrong and you can't pay the debt back.

If you're carrying debt, go to MoneyMachineResources.com and download the Debt Breakthrough Calculator to get yourself on a detailed debt paydown plan.

7. **Infringement and Theft.** There are two directions that this risk can come from. First, let's consider someone who might infringe on your work through duplication, plagiarism, or outright theft. Some of this can be mitigated through structuring and getting the proper protections in place, like patents, trademarks, and copyrights. The other risk is being on the other end—accused of being the infringer. Make sure your work is yours and yours alone.

8. **Litigation.** There's always some general litigation risk, which can come from within your business operations (internal) or from outside (external).

The following risks are more relevant to business dealings:

9. **Business Partnerships.** It's a rare thing that partnerships work out over the long term. Just like a romantic relationship, any type of partnership could break up. The other person's values may shift, or their vision may change. At that point, there's a business divorce coming. I say that if you don't need the other person's money or their mind (knowledge), then you don't need the partnership. Just because you're friends doesn't mean you should be partners.

   The other thing to consider is the nuance that your partner brings to your life from a risk-exposure standpoint. They potentially can do things in the business that make *you* personally liable—like causing accidents, taking on debt, or other actions. Also, if a partner gets sick, becomes disabled, goes through divorce, or even dies, it puts an additional burden on the business and your future if you aren't clear about how to handle it. Some of these risks are insurable; others are not. But all should be specifically dealt with in a detailed, *written* partnership agreement— *NO HANDSHAKES.*

10. **Professional Mistakes.** Let's face it, we're all human and can make honest mistakes. You may give wrong or erroneous advice. When this happens, the first thing is to try to make it right. Second, you can typically insure this risk through some type of errors and omissions (E&O) or professional liability coverage. Certain professionals, such as doctors, are required to carry this type of insurance.

11. **Employee Related.** This could be anything from an employee getting into an accident or getting hurt on the job. It can also include suits for wrongful termination, breach of duty, and even sexual harassment. Remember to do the right thing and treat people with respect. After that, most of these can be insured against with a liability policy, workers' comp policy, or other type of insurance. Some are required to have in most states, such as workers' comp.

12. **Product Liability.** This is when something goes wrong with your product and someone is injured physically or mentally. It's an insurable risk.

Beyond the Dirty Dozen Dream Killers, there's one other devil that we all deal with: taxes.

TAXES: THE UNAVOIDABLE HOUSEHOLD CHORES

When it comes to taxes, we all know they're a fact of life, right? They're like the unavoidable household chores. But think about it: you can get taxed by as much as 50 percent or more on your income, which means it can be one of the biggest destroyers of your wealth. Yes, you need to pay your taxes, but no, you don't need to *overpay* them.

While I certainly don't expect you to be a tax expert, I do think it's important to understand some of the basics and rely on good experts to educate and guide you. Reducing your taxes always starts with keeping accurate records. But as you grow, having a skilled tax advisor in your corner will be a game changer for you and your money. They will help you stay up-to-date on tax laws and regulations that apply to you. More important, they will help you be proactive with tax planning so you can minimize your liabilities, keep more of your hard-earned money, and reduce your probability of audit.

Now let me share some more specific tips on how to stay on top of taxes and protect your wealth.

Understand Deductions and Credits

First, understand the rules of engagement. Simply understanding how the tax system works and what the difference is between a deduction and a credit can go a long way toward understanding how to reduce your tax burden.

The way to think about a tax deduction is that it's like getting a discount on your tax bill—it's a percentage off the amount due. A credit is like having a gift card. The amount of the gift card offsets the tax, dollar for dollar. Ignorance or naivete in this area is not your friend. It can lead to overpaying your taxes or, worse, an audit or landing in tax court. And I don't have to tell you that none of that is going to feel good or put more money in your pocket.

Here's the way I look at it: If I'm going to pay taxes at, say, 25 percent, then every legal deduction I can take means that the government is subsidizing them to the tune of 25 percent. Well, I want to make sure the government picks up their full portion of the bill. For example, if I were to buy a computer for my business for $1,000 and I was able to deduct it on my taxes, it would reduce my income by $1,000. And if my tax rate were 25 percent, then this deduction would reduce my taxes by $250. In the end, after the tax savings, the computer cost me only $750 instead of $1,000. This is why everything you can legally deduct becomes a huge value to you.

This is a visual of how it would play out if there were any tax credits you could use to offset your taxes.

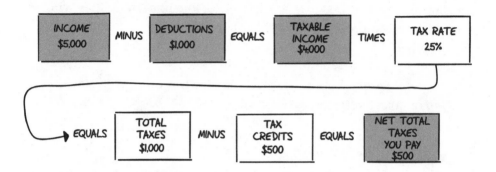

To make sure the government pays their portion of the bill, it's important to keep track of all your income, expenses, deductions, and credits. Good recordkeeping is the foundation of effective tax management. This should be something a bit more sophisticated than receipts in a shoebox. You can use any number of software options to help you out. You could even hire a bookkeeper if the task seems too complicated.

Seek Professional Advice

Second, don't be afraid to ask for help to increase your understanding. Tax laws and regulations can be super complicated. Heck, I remember a friend of mine who was a United States Tax Court judge, and he said that there are two things you never want to watch being made: sausage and tax law.

So, talk to tax professionals like certified public accountants (CPAs) that specialize in tax strategy and planning. But here's the deal: you want someone that knows their stuff but is also willing to educate you so you're better equipped to make more powerful decisions for your taxes. Also, you want someone who is proactive, not reactive. This means that they have regular, scheduled planning meetings with you, and they reach out if and when there are tax changes that could impact you. Too often, the professionals in this space are reactive and passive, driven by the deadlines instead of forethought and responsiveness. Be critical when evaluating whom you work with. After all, they work for you and with you, and you can define the relationship you want, not the other way around. Effectively, they need to earn the right to have you as a client.

Consider the Tax Implications of Each Investment

Other things that can impact your taxes are the types of investments you make and where you make them. Investment taxes can have a huge impact on your returns. So, as you build your wealth, think through the tax implications of each investment so you don't get blindsided with a tax bill you didn't expect.

For instance, making investments through a 401(k), IRA, Roth IRA, or HSA has the ability to shield you from taxes today or in the future (in the case of a Roth). Also, holding assets for more than one year allows you to get taxed at a maximum of 20 percent rather than your regular income tax rate, which could go as high as 50 percent depending on your state.

Now, let me be clear on this, though: any investment *must* be a good investment on its own merits, not because of the tax benefits. You should never make an investment in something solely because of the tax elements. A tax professional or financial advisor can help you create a tax-efficient investment plan that aligns with your financial goals. (You'll learn more about the different types of advisors later in this book.)

Implement Tax-Loss Harvesting

Last, consider implementing tax-loss harvesting to minimize capital gains taxes on your investments. Tax-loss harvesting is when people decide to sell the investments that have lost money on purpose, so they can use the loss to help lower their taxes by offsetting gains from other investments. They typically replace the sold investments with new ones, hoping the new ones will grow in value while at the same time saving them on taxes. There are special rules that apply to this strategy that you need to be aware of and careful of. Get guidance from a financial advisor.

Your financial advisor should be proactively bringing these types of strategies to you and helping you use them effectively when it makes sense in your situation.

There's so much more here that we could talk about, but my job in this section is to raise your awareness and give you some guidance in going deeper on what could apply to you in trying to reduce your taxes to the lowest legally possible amount.

CHAPTER 18

MASTERING THE ART OF SAFEGUARDING YOUR WEALTH

We need to vigilantly stand guard at the gates of our legacy.

— MEL ABRAHAM

You know, protecting your financial assets is kind of like building a fortress around your hard-earned wealth. It's essential to keep an eye on potential risks and work to eliminate or reduce them. So, let's talk about the four-step framework to secure your financial future.

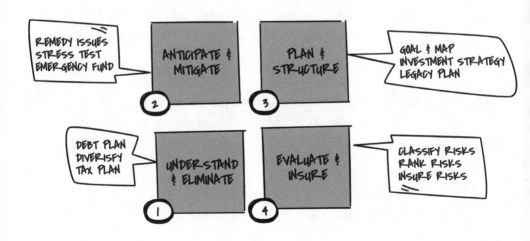

STEP 1: UNDERSTAND AND ELIMINATE RISKS

First, let's identify possible risks. We've got to deep dive into our current financial situation and figure out any weak spots that might threaten our wealth. You've got the Dirty Dozen Dream Killers from the previous chapter, but let's point out three common risks:

- **Excessive debt.** High levels of debt can lead to financial instability and put your assets at risk. Work toward paying off debt and maintaining a manageable debt-to-income ratio.

- **Lack of diversification.** A concentrated investment portfolio exposes you to higher risk. Diversify your investments across different asset classes and sectors to minimize potential losses.

- **Tax liabilities.** Understand your tax obligations and work with a tax professional to minimize your tax burden and ensure compliance with all relevant regulations.

STEP 2: ANTICIPATE AND MITIGATE POTENTIAL ISSUES

Next, we should anticipate and tackle potential issues that could pop up down the road and fix them. This may include doing the following:

- Look for possible problems and hazards before they become problems, and solve them. Here's an example of what I mean. When I'm doing my live events, one thing I do is walk the event space to look for issues like trip hazards. These could be loose staging or cables on the floor, or any number of other things. I have the problem fixed before anyone ever sets foot into the space.

- Regularly review and stress test your financial plan. Stress testing your financial plan means checking how strong your money bridge is for when unexpected things happen. For example, what if you suddenly needed to pay for a big expense that pops up, like a big home repair? Or, what would happen to your plan and investments if a recession hit or the stock market dropped 20 percent? Stress testing means running many different scenarios to see how they impact your numbers. You'll see if your financial plan is strong enough to handle these surprises. If it isn't, you can make strategic changes to your plan before anything like that hits. This will keep you from getting blindsided if the economy or your job changes, because with the stress testing you are seeing what would happen to your financial situation if things didn't go as planned. It also allows you to account for changes in your life circumstances, market conditions, and financial goals.

- As we discussed in Chapter 12, establish an emergency fund to cover unexpected expenses such as medical bills, job loss, or urgent home repairs. Having a good emergency fund that is liquid and available can give you a ton of peace of mind— which, as you know, is why I like to call it a Peace of Mind Fund.

STEP 3: PLAN AND STRUCTURE YOUR FINANCES

Now, let's talk about structuring your finances, which we've focused on a lot in this book. Key elements of a comprehensive financial plan include

- a clear understanding of your financial goals and a road map for achieving them;

- a savings and investment strategy tailored to your risk tolerance, time horizon, and objectives;

- a detailed outline of your income, expenses, and financial priorities, allowing you to make informed decisions about spending and saving according to your money purpose statement and Affluence Vision;

- estate planning to ensure that your assets are distributed according to your wishes and that your loved ones are taken care of in the event of your death; and

- a financial team that can help you navigate the road ahead.

The three key advisors everyone should have in their corner are:

- **Financial advisor.** They help you create a comprehensive financial plan, provide you with investment recommendations, and keep you accountable to your financial goals.

- **Tax advisor.** They help you minimize your tax liabilities by recommending tax-efficient investment strategies and ensuring you take advantage of all available tax deductions and credits.

- **Legal advisor.** They assist you with estate planning, asset protection, and other legal matters related to your finances, ensuring your wealth is protected for generations to come.

One key aspect to understand when selecting a financial advisor is the difference between the *fiduciary standard* and the *suitability standard.*

Fiduciary advisors are legally required to act in the best interest of their clients, putting their clients' interests above their own. They must disclose any conflicts of interest and are held to a higher ethical standard.

On the other hand, advisors operating under the *suitability* standard are required only to recommend investments that are suitable for their clients based on their financial situation and objectives. Note that they are *not* required to put their clients' interests above their own, potentially leading to conflicts of interest.

When selecting a financial advisor, it's crucial to seek out those who operate under the fiduciary standard, as they are more likely to provide unbiased advice that truly benefits you.

Additionally, be sure to ask potential advisors about their investment philosophy, approach to financial planning, and how they handle conflicts of interest. This information will help you determine whether an advisor is a good fit for your unique financial situation and goals.

When interviewing potential financial advisors, some key questions to ask include:

- Are you a fiduciary?
- What are your credentials and certifications?
- Can you provide references from current clients?
- How do you get paid (e.g., fee-based, commission-based, or a combination)?
- Do you have any potential conflicts of interest?

By asking these questions, you can gain a better understanding of an advisor's commitment to their clients and their overall approach to wealth management.

STEP 4: INSURE AGAINST UNFORESEEN EVENTS

Finally, let's chat about insurance. It plays a crucial role in protecting our financial assets from life's curveballs, like accidents, illnesses, or natural disasters. Make sure you've got the right coverage in place, whether it's life insurance, disability insurance, property and casualty insurance, or liability insurance.

- **Classify risks.** Take the time to create a list of the possible risks that still exist after you've done everything you can to eliminate or mitigate them.

- **Rank risks.** Rank the risks based on how much the exposure might be and what the probability is of each risk happening.

- **Insure risks.** Get the appropriate amount of insurance to take care of you and your financial future.

To help you out, here are the different types of insurance to consider and how I think about them.

— **Auto insurance.** Legally, this is a required insurance in the vast majority of states—and a good idea to have even in those states that don't require it. As someone with wealth, you should get higher limits well beyond the minimums.

— **Homeowners'/renters' insurance.** This policy insures your home and its contents. It also provides your base personal liability coverage for any personal liability claims that may come up.

— **Health insurance.** Health care can be one of the most costly expenses as you age. This insurance, although expensive, is a must-have. The whole medical and health-insurance industry is a convoluted and complicated space to navigate at times. But what isn't complicated is the fact that you need it. Medical bills are often cited as the biggest cause for bankruptcy in the United States.[1]

— **Umbrella insurance.** This is a secondary liability policy to cover any claims that are beyond your auto and home liability coverages. It's relatively inexpensive because "secondary" means it pays out only after your other policies are exhausted first. It is a great overall policy to have to keep you safe beyond what you can get on your regular auto or homeowners' policies. There are both personal and business policies available, and it is important to know the inclusions, criteria, and exclusions of all policies before signing up.

— **Disability insurance.** We discussed this earlier, and I think long-term disability insurance is a must-have, especially if you're the primary income-source provider. I believe that most people are better off having a long-term disability insurance policy and a well-funded Peace of Mind Fund rather than having short-term disability insurance.

— **Long-term care insurance.** This policy is for those who may one day have a need for long-term care. While you might not expect to use it until you're older than 65, you could start considering purchasing a policy in your 50s when premiums are more affordable.[2] This is separate from your actual health insurance, which you still need. Annual long-term care costs can range from $54,000 (assisted living) to as high as $108,405 (nursing home).[3] I know from personal experience how much it costs, because my 90-year-old mom needs a lot of care in an assisted living facility and needs dialysis three times a week. This puts her monthly costs at $17,000 *per month*. This can force you to receive substandard care, not receive care, or quickly destroy you financially if you don't plan for it or have enough assets to fund it. That's when this type of insurance can help.

— **Identity theft insurance.** With cybercrimes on the rise, having a policy that will cover the damages and pay to fix your credit is a good idea. Many homeowners' and renters' insurance policies offer this coverage as a rider. However, I personally purchased a separate policy because my homeowners insurance didn't offer as much coverage as I was comfortable with.

— **Life insurance.** Let me be clear here: Life insurance is *not* meant to make your heirs wealthy. It's meant to take care of outstanding obligations and bills when you pass away and also to replace the income you were bringing in so that your heirs can continue their accustomed lifestyle. It would supplement any income being generated from your investable assets (Money Machine). If you've fully funded your Money Machine, you might not need this insurance, but you should certainly consider it during the wealth-building process.

Unless there's some unusual need, I recommend *only* a term policy for this use. These policies are for a set period of time and offer higher benefits for lower premium costs. You are simply paying for insurance for the time you need it. There are no investments or other elements involved. They are far less complex and way less costly than permanent life insurance. You might choose a length of time that covers you until your kids are grown up or the house is paid off, for example. At the end of the term, coverage ends and there is no cash value returned to you.

There are many salespeople out there promoting whole-life, permanent-life, or universal-life insurance due to their having a cash value that you can withdraw or borrow from during your lifetime. However, these are basically partly insurance and partly investment policies that are not very good at playing either part. They're typically much more expensive than term policies for less coverage and don't offer a good return on your investment. Generally, avoid these. Remember that the only tool that an insurance salesperson has in their tool chest is an insurance policy, so of course they'll find a way to make it right for your situation.

I'm sure that last statement will piss off many insurance agents, but I'm not here to make friends. I'm here to help you make the right decisions and choices for your needs without the bias of a big, fat commission.

Bottom line: if you buy life insurance, do not use anything but term. Insurance is meant to be just that—insurance—and *not* a wrapper for an investment.

Other insurances I typically avoid are:

- Credit life and disability
- Cancer and hospital indemnity
- Accidental death
- Prepaid burial policies

- Mortgage life insurance
- Policies with fancy options: return of premium and waiver of premium

Note: I have additional information about business-related insurances in Appendix E. For more details, visit my website at MoneyMachineResources.com.

By following this four-step approach to financial protection, you can effectively safeguard your wealth and ensure a secure and prosperous financial future. Remember, the key to financial success is not just about growing your wealth but also about protecting it from potential risks, losses, and setbacks.

Part IV

LIVE THE JOURNEY

No dream is so big that it can't be finished.

— MEL ABRAHAM

CHAPTER 19

BUILDING YOUR MONEY MACHINE

A rich life is built on the things that money can't buy.

— MEL ABRAHAM

Hopefully by now, you realize that this book and your financial journey aren't just about money. They're about so much more. This is about your life. It's about your vision. It's about your children and the generations beyond them. It's about your legacy. It's about your mission and the movements that matter to you.

It's about living into the legacy you were put here to live, to live fully expressed into the gifts you've been given—and to be an example of possibility for all who see you and how you show up in your world.

That's exactly why you're building a Money Machine! It's like a self-sustaining, wealth-generating system that can be passed down and grow over time. I think about it in my life. I created a machine that allows my wife, Stefanie, and me to live into the vision we have for our lives together. Then when, God forbid, I'm gone, the machine takes care of her for the rest of her days. Once she decides her time here is done, the machine will pass on to Jeremy and Kamie to take care of them and our granddaughters (Emily and Aria).

When the Money Machine is built the right way, as we discussed in depth throughout Part III, this process will go on for generations and generations. You effectively become the inflection point of change for your whole family tree.

To make sure your Money Machine will be able to sustain itself over time, let's break down what you should do from here to make this your reality.

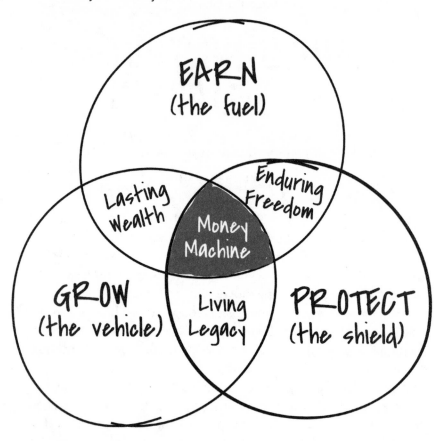

STEP 1: ESTABLISH AN UNSHAKABLE MONEY MACHINE FOUNDATION

First, you need an unshakable foundation in the form of a well-structured financial plan, tailored to a vivid vision that you created. However, you build and fuel the plan by first maximizing your value to optimize your income. Remember, you aren't just looking for a single stream of income but developing multiple sources of income that leverage your time—in other words, you're able to bring in increasing levels of income with less direct effort on your part. Your plan will be informed by your risk tolerance, capacity, and time horizon and built through the Wealth Priority Ladder. The cool thing is that with a process like this, the tools you have now make you better equipped to navigate and adjust regularly as things change in your life and the financial markets.

Key elements of your financial plan should include

- a clear understanding of your financial objectives and milestones, such as retirement savings, education funding, and wealth accumulation;

- a diversified investment portfolio that balances growth and income-generating assets to minimize risk and maximize returns; and

- a strong focus on asset protection and estate planning to ensure the preservation and efficient transfer of your wealth to future generations.

STEP 2: BUILD YOUR MONEY MACHINE COMPONENTS

Now you're ready to build the components of your Money Machine. Think of them as the gears that work together to generate income, appreciation, and wealth accumulation. Remember that the magic in the Money Machine is when you get your money to work harder for you than you did for it. There will come a time when your Money Machine will actually generate more income on a regular basis than you are by actively working.

I'm talking about leveraged income streams (e.g., dividend-paying stocks, rental properties, royalties, and annuities), growth assets (e.g,. real estate, stocks, and innovative companies), and preservation strategies to protect your capital from erosion due to inflation, taxes, and market volatility.

Key components of your Money Machine include:

- **Leveraged income streams.** These are sources of income that require little to no ongoing effort on your part, such as dividend-paying stocks, rental properties, royalties, and annuities. These income streams will provide ongoing cash flow to sustain your Money Machine and support your financial goals.

- **Growth assets.** Invest in assets with high growth potential, such as real estate, stocks, and innovative companies. These assets will appreciate over time and contribute to the overall growth of your Money Machine.

- **Capital preservation strategies.** Implement strategies to protect your capital from erosion due to inflation, taxes, and market volatility. This may include investing in inflation-protected securities, tax-efficient investments, and diversifying your portfolio across different asset classes and sectors.

STEP 3: OPTIMIZE YOUR MONEY MACHINE

To ensure your Money Machine operates efficiently and generates the desired level of wealth and income, it's essential to continuously optimize its performance. This involves monitoring your investments, adjusting your strategies as needed, and staying informed about financial markets and economic trends. Consider the following actions to optimize your Money Machine:

- Regularly review your financial plan and investment strategies to ensure they remain aligned with your goals and risk tolerance. I recommend once per quarter at a minimum (especially when starting out). These include certain metrics to make sure you are on plan. The metrics will change based on your plan and your investments. The easiest way is to have a one-page scorecard with the relevant metrics at your fingertips. I've included a sample of mine.

- Conduct ongoing research and due diligence to identify new investment opportunities and potential risks that may impact your Money Machine's performance.
- Consult with financial professionals, such as financial planners, tax advisors, and estate-planning attorneys to obtain expert guidance and insights that can help you make informed decisions and enhance your Money Machine's effectiveness.

MEANINGFUL METRIC	MONTH #1	MONTH #2	MONTH #3
Cash			
Total Net Worth			
Investable Net Worth			
Savings Rate			
Asset Allocation Cash ETFs/Indexes Stocks Bonds Alternatives			
Portfolio Returns			
Expense Ratio			
Total Debt			
Asset Location After Tax Pre Tax Taxable			

STEP 4: PLAN FOR PASSING ON YOUR LEGACY

Finally, it's crucial to plan for the eventual transfer of your Money Machine to your heirs or chosen beneficiaries. Proper estate planning will ensure the smooth and efficient transfer of your wealth, minimizing taxes and preserving your legacy for future generations.

Key aspects of estate planning should include

- drafting a will or establishing a trust to dictate the distribution of your assets upon your death;

- designating beneficiaries for your financial accounts and insurance policies;

- establishing a succession plan for any businesses or real estate holdings you may own; and

- regularly reviewing and updating your estate plan to account for changes in your life circumstances, financial goals, and applicable laws and regulations.

By diligently building and optimizing your Money Machine, you'll create a lasting legacy that can provide financial security and prosperity for your family and future generations. As you embark on this journey, remember that building a successful Money Machine takes time, patience, and ongoing effort. But the reward of leaving a legacy that endures for generations makes the investment well worth it.

Incorporating Philanthropy and Social Impact in Your Money Machine

One of the greatest gifts of living a rich life is that you can be even more generous than you were before to the causes and movements that matter to you. Your Money Machine plays a significant role in supporting charitable causes and creating a positive social impact. By incorporating philanthropy into your financial plan, you can extend your legacy beyond your family, benefiting your community and the wider world.

There are several ways to incorporate philanthropy into your Money Machine:

- Establish a charitable trust or foundation that supports causes and organizations aligned with your values and priorities.

- Include charitable giving in your estate plan, designating a portion of your wealth to be donated to your chosen causes upon your death.

- Use your investment strategies to promote positive social and environmental outcomes, such as investing in socially responsible or impact-focused funds.

Educating Your Heirs and Beneficiaries

A crucial aspect of passing on your legacy is educating your heirs and beneficiaries about financial management, investment strategies, and the principles that underlie your Money Machine. By doing so, you empower them to take ownership of the legacy you've built and continue to grow and preserve it for future generations. Consider the following methods to educate your heirs and beneficiaries:

- Involve them in your financial planning process, providing insight into your investment strategies, financial goals, and risk-management techniques.

- Share your experiences, successes, and failures in building your Money Machine, imparting valuable lessons and wisdom.

- Encourage them to pursue their financial education by reading books, attending workshops, or working with financial professionals.

- Foster a mindset of financial stewardship, emphasizing the importance of preserving and growing the family's wealth for the benefit of future generations.

* * *

Now, I get it, this may seem like a lot to do, but here's the good news: You don't need to get it all done today. It's really like building a house. You start with the foundation or the few elements that you need now, and nothing more. It may be getting your Comfort Fund in place or building your investments. Follow the Wealth Priority Ladder as your key to what to do each step of the way.

As you move through the process, you'll layer on each next step until you build the Money Machine you need to give you the life you desire and deserve.

This allows you to live a "get to" life instead of a "have to" life—where you do what you want, when you want, and how you want. Yours becomes a life driven by options and choice.

But wait, you're not done yet!

You need to keep your Money Machine running smoothly and efficiently. As I noted earlier, that means monitoring your investments, adjusting your strategies when needed, and staying informed about financial markets and economic trends. The good part is, you won't be doing this alone—because you'll have the right team and guidance in place to help you out on the journey.

Last, imagine for a moment the kind of indelible impact you could leave by fully living into what you were meant to be. Think of the fact that you can pass on your newly acquired financial skills and the Money Machine to live beyond you and carry your impact for generations to come. And since that's the case, I can't complete this book and journey without giving you one of the most important rules of all: Skill Sets before Assets. For your machine to create a generational impact, you *must* make sure that those who handle it after you're gone know exactly *what* to do and *how*.

CHAPTER 20

SKILL SETS BEFORE ASSETS

You can be the financial inflection point for your whole family tree.

— MEL ABRAHAM

Back in 2006, I had two brothers come to me after their mother passed away. At the time, they were worth just over $5 million. They wanted me to guide them so they could preserve their wealth and grow it for their future. Here's the thing, though . . . in my conversations with them, I found out that when their dad passed away five years earlier, the family had been worth $180 million. I almost fell out of my chair as I heard this. Where the heck did $175 million go in five years? Think about this: $180 million invested at 5 percent will give you $750,000 *each month* without you ever touching the $180 million. How does this happen?

I often see this pattern in families: We get so focused on acquiring, achieving, accumulating, and passing on assets that we never think about the right way to pass them on. I have a hugely important rule for this . . . *never* pass on assets before passing on *skill sets*!

If the heirs are unwilling to grow, then the assets need to go. You want your assets to go where they're going to serve the best. If your heirs are not good stewards of the thing you built, then it's not their right to have them.

Frankly, I feel so strongly about this rule that if I didn't feel that Jeremy would be a good steward of the Money Machine when we're gone, I would give it all to charities or other causes.

I can't stress this enough. By equipping your beneficiaries with essential financial skills, you give them the tools they need to not only manage the wealth you leave them but also to grow it for generations to come so your Money Machine lives on.

HOW TO PASS ON THE SKILL SETS

Now, the rule I just laid down may sound self-serving, but I suggest it because I think you and your heirs *must* be on the same page. You all need to play from the same playbook. So, with that, one of the first things I recommend is to have them read *this* book. This will make sure you're all working from a common set of principles, rules, and tools.

The other thing to do early on is to bring them on the financial journey with you. Too often, heirs are simply spectators in the financial game. Then, when they're called to get on the field, they have no clue what to do, how to act, or—and this is even more important—how to think.

There are a few ways I brought Jeremy along on my journey over the years:

- I started talking with him about money and financial stuff early on, and I actually gave him a "commission" starting at age 10. I call it that instead of an "allowance" because he needed to learn to earn. This allowed me to teach him about creating value for others, the value of a dollar, and the importance of money management.

- He used the money he made from me to pay for school lunches and some of his toys, but also to save and invest and be generous to charities that he liked.

- I would do a match on his big purchases or his investments. He would always have to make the first move, and then I would step in with him. So when it came to buying his first car, he saved half of the down payment and then I matched it. When it came to funding his first investment or IRA, I matched his contribution.

- I showed him the impact of debt on his ability to invest as well as the magic of compounding when he did invest.

Doing little things like this over time opens up the conversations with your heirs at a higher level so you can instill in them your values, thoughts, and strategies. They aren't left to their own devices, and you get to watch them grow and flourish.

THE CRITICAL SKILL SETS

I think one of the greatest gifts a parent can give to their kids is the set of skills to be financially independent, responsible adults with good values. Besides, then you mitigate your risk of their knocking on your door at midlife, wanting their old room back because they weren't properly equipped to handle money on their own. (While there are many reasons some people might desire a multigenerational household, nobody wants to be forced into one due to lack of choice and resources!)

More specifically, there are some critical skills you can focus on beyond this book. These skills can be developed over years as you work with your heirs early on like I did.

- **Financial literacy.** First and foremost, financial literacy is key. By raising your heirs' financial literacy, you build their financial muscle to be able to carry the wealth forward. It's all about making sure your beneficiaries have a strong foundation in budgeting, saving, investing, and risk management. They should understand the power of time in wealth building and the importance of making smart decisions, because now they know the long-term impact of their choices. So, encourage them to read some books, go to seminars, and check out some online resources. (You might even make this a *requirement* for them to be included in your plan!) And, of course, introduce them to financial professionals who can give them expert insights and guidance. With a solid financial literacy foundation, they'll be able to make informed decisions that keep their finances in check and contribute to a legacy that lasts.

- **Emotional intelligence.** There's no arguing that money can be an emotional topic. For this reason, emotional intelligence is key to wealth building and management. Rarely, if ever, are emotional money decisions good ones. Basically, it's all about being able to recognize, understand, and manage emotions (both your own and others'). When it comes to financial decision-making, emotional intelligence helps your beneficiaries stay calm and levelheaded, avoiding impulsive decisions fueled by fear or greed. Teach them some self-awareness, empathy, and emotional regulation techniques like mindfulness and meditation to help them stay cool and focused when the going gets tough. Having a proven system based on time-tested principles to follow helps take the emotions out of it too.

- **General business acumen.** Next up is general business acumen for must-have skills to build and manage assets. By homing in on these skills, your beneficiaries can create new income streams, optimize their investments, and navigate the complexities of the business world. Encourage them to get some education and training in business-related fields, network with successful entrepreneurs, and start or invest in ventures that align with their interests and financial goals.

- **Risk management.** Of course, effective risk management is essential for preserving and growing your assets. Teach your beneficiaries how to identify, assess, and mitigate risks associated with their assets. Help them establish a risk-management framework that outlines their risk tolerance, assessment processes, and mitigation strategies. Staying adaptable to changing circumstances and evolving risks is key, so make sure they regularly review and update their plan.

- **Communication and relationship building.** Strong communication and relationship-building skills are also critical for managing a financial legacy. These skills allow your beneficiaries to engage with financial professionals, negotiate favorable terms, and foster collaboration among family members and stakeholders. Encourage them to practice active listening, develop negotiation skills, and cultivate a network of trusted professionals and peers who can provide support and advice.

- **Adaptability and continuous learning.** The financial landscape is always changing, so adaptability and continuous learning are crucial. Teach your beneficiaries to stay up-to-date with market trends, technological advancements, and new investment opportunities. Encourage them to embrace new technologies and tools that can streamline their financial management and open up new avenues for wealth building. And remind them to revise their financial strategies as circumstances change, as well as to learn from their mistakes and experiences.

- **Legacy planning and wealth transfer.** Finally, legacy planning and wealth transfer are key concepts to pass on. Make sure your beneficiaries understand how to create a comprehensive plan that minimizes tax liabilities, preserves assets, and provides for *their* family members and the causes they care about. Help them familiarize themselves with estate-planning concepts like wills, trusts, and powers of attorney. Introduce them to estate-planning professionals who can create a customized legacy plan that meets their needs and goals. And, most important, encourage open communication within the family so everyone understands your intentions and is prepared to manage the wealth you leave behind.

* * *

Phew, that was a lot! Just know that by teaching your loved ones these essential skills, you're setting them up for long-term success in managing the assets you pass on to them. It's not just about the assets themselves but also passing on the knowledge, skills, and mindset that underlie your wealth-building journey. So, keep on sharing the wealth of knowledge (literally and figuratively), and you'll ensure that your financial legacy can be effectively managed and preserved for generations to come!

CHAPTER 21

THE LEGACY FACTOR

Always strive to live a life that outlives you!

— MEL ABRAHAM

All right, folks, we've covered some essential skills for building and managing assets, but now it's time to talk about the bigger picture. Sure, creating a Money Machine is great for securing your financial future and taking care of your loved ones, but it really is about more than that. It's about living in a way that is fully expressed and contributes to the greater good of life and the world around us.

Think about it—when you have financial freedom, you're more free to make a positive impact on society, your community, and the causes you care about. You get to support local businesses, donate to charities, and invest in sustainable initiatives. By using your Money Machine for good, the benefits reach way further than just you and your loved ones. You become the catalyst that causes a ripple effect of positive change in the world. This is what I call the Legacy Factor™.

WHAT IS LEGACY?

One day, shortly after Stefanie and I met, she saw me giving a keynote presentation to an audience of about a thousand folks. One of the themes in my talk was living in possibility and creating a legacy. This was within weeks of us meeting, so she didn't really know me too well. Being from Philly, she thought that when I spoke of legacy, I wanted some statue erected of me somewhere like the one of Rocky Balboa by the steps of the Philadelphia Museum of Art.

I totally get it; people usually talk about legacy only in the context of dying and what we leave behind. But no, I don't want a statue or my name on a plaque on some building. (Although I did tell her I was going to have a statue of me put in the house after I'm gone so she wouldn't forget me!) To me, legacy is much smaller but far greater than something like that.

First, I don't believe legacy is created at death. I believe legacy is created in the moment. Every moment we have that we can impact someone's life is a moment that creates legacy, because that person is forever changed. So in effect, you are living your legacy each and every day by stacking the moments daily. These moments, as simple as a kind word or gesture, can change the direction of someone's life, creating a lasting impact. When you realize that each moment has the power to change and create legacy, I think we then give each moment the presence and reverence it deserves. There are no inconsequential moments.

Like I said earlier, there's a gap between how good we are today and how good we're capable of being. To bridge this gap, we must strive to be the best version of ourselves, living fully expressed lives. When we do, we create a life that outlives us.

But how do we achieve this?

THE THREE PILLARS OF THE LEGACY FACTOR

The Legacy Factor is a framework that helps you close the gap between how good you are today and how good you are capable of being. It's driven by three critical outcomes—being highly valued (whether in your career, relationships, community, or society), creating a lasting impact (where you have a positive impact that lasts beyond the moment), and having resolute integrity (doing what you say you're going to do and living by your word).

Accomplishing these three critical outcomes is built on three distinct pillars:

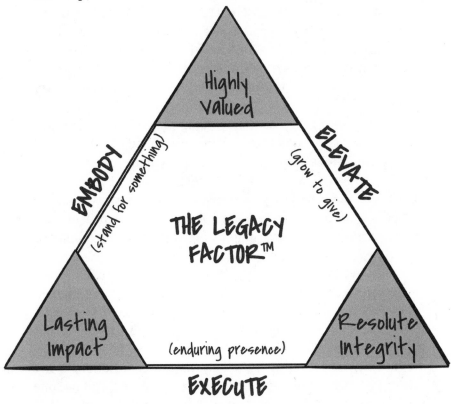

Pillar #1: Embody. What Do You Stand For?

To *embody* is to move from being a participant in life to a trailblazer. It's about understanding what you stand for and allowing your unique identity to emerge. It doesn't matter where we start or what we have; it's about what we do with it.

Unshakable values and bold courage are essential elements for embodying your legacy. They help you take risks, stand up for what is right, and show up in life.

I've always been a firm believer that we have the power to shape our own lives into the masterpieces we envision. It reminds me of an interesting story about the famous sculpture Michelangelo's

David.[1] You might be surprised to know that he was not the original sculptor commissioned for the project.

Agostino di Duccio, a student of the famed Donatello, was the first sculptor who laid hands on the marble. He abandoned the project after a few years, having done little work on it. The committee then turned to Antonio Rossellino, who turned down the project almost immediately because, he said, the marble was poor in quality.

For 25 long years, that same piece of marble lay exposed to the elements, untouched and unappreciated. That is, until Michelangelo came along and didn't allow where he was starting to define where he would end up. He effectively created one of the most recognizable statues in history out of what was said to be a poor-quality piece of marble. By living in alignment with your core beliefs, you can shape your existence into a masterpiece that you can truly be proud of.

Let's revisit my dad's story again for a moment . . . Imagine that you're a teenager, living in a country where you're being hunted for your beliefs. You live in fear that you'll be hanged in the square because of what you stand for—but people need protecting and that's all that matters to you.

The Farhud in Iraq in 1941 had my dad and many others living in fear. In 1946, when he was only 17 years old, my dad became part of a group called the Five Mavericks that helped people escape to safety and protected those who stayed in the country. But two of his comrades got caught and were being tortured to get the names of the other three. They wanted to make an example of the five of them. My dad and the other two helped the captured men escape, then used fake papers to flee the country. Eventually my dad made his way to the United States, started a family, and built a strong foundation for future generations of Abrahams to thrive.

Fast-forward to four days before my dad passed away. I was sitting with him and asked, "You knew that if they caught you, they would hang you in the square. You were seventeen years old. Why would you do something like that?"

Sitting in that wheelchair, as strong as I've ever seen him, he said, "Because it was the right thing to do."

My dad made a decision in 1946 without knowing the years-long impact of that decision. It became an inflection point that changed all our lives. What seemed like the right thing in the moment created a family, a heritage, something that will last for decades. The legacy he created isn't what he left *for* me; the legacy was what he left *in* me and how he showed up every day.

My dad had a set of values that were always dictated by what was the *right thing* to do, even if it put him in harm's way or in a situation in which he could lose everything. It drove what he did all his life, and what I did all my life

And that leads me to the next factor of this pillar: bold courage. Bold courage is how you show up in life. Too often, we're ready to quit because we don't realize that we have something left in us.

When I owned my martial arts studio, our black belt tests were four and a half hours long. They were grueling, as the students had to work their techniques and were sparring the entire length of time. Then the final segment of the test was to spar me for three minutes. This was after they were completely exhausted from the previous four hours of testing.

The students came into the test thinking it was four and a half hours long. But in reality, the true test was the three minutes with me at a point where they had nothing left. It was about them reaching deep down to find it in themselves when things got tough.

It all became clear for them when I explained, "You were at a point where you didn't have anything left and could go no further. But you did!

"I know that at some point in your life, you'll end up in a situation where you say you can't go any further—just like you felt here. But now you know there is more in you. Let this be your first reference to know you can keep going."

What I know is that you need to be willing to take risks, because without risk, you can't grow. The greatest hazard in life is not to risk anything at all. The person who risks nothing does nothing, has nothing, and becomes nothing.

So, where in your life can you show bold courage and take a risk? Remember that nothing we do is terminal. We can always learn, feel, change, grow, and love.

This is a great time to examine your life and look for something that you've always wanted to do or considered doing but have backed away from out of fear, discomfort, or even lack of know-how. It should be something that requires you to muster a bit of courage to move through. What's the first step you need to take? Schedule that step within the next 14 days.

Pillar #2: Elevate. How Do You Inspire and Influence?

This brings me to the second aspect of the Legacy Factor: *elevate*. Once we embody our core values, we need to focus on how we can grow and give back. Elevation is all about expanding our limits, transforming from limited to limitless. If we don't elevate, we can't create the impact we're meant to have in the world. We need to be continuously growing, giving, and putting our best out there.

To elevate, we need to do a few things. First, we must escalate our skills (like we discussed in the Skill Up, Value Up section in Chapter 11), improve our ability to serve, and do more. We must be in a constant state of growth, setting intentional goals for the results we want to achieve. Most important, we need to practice meaningful generosity, focusing on *becoming* more rather than merely acquiring more.

It's worth noting that 71 percent of employees want their companies to contribute positively to social or environmental causes, and roughly 75 percent of consumers expect companies to address important social issues.[2] Profits should be a byproduct of the service we provide and the work we do, not the sole objective.

To truly elevate, we must find ways to contribute to the world beyond our businesses and our own success. This means giving back to the community, working on social and environmental issues, and making a positive impact in the lives of others. This is where true fulfillment and growth come from.

One example of a company that has successfully elevated is Patagonia, the outdoor clothing and gear company. Founded by Yvon Chouinard in 1973, Patagonia has always been committed to environmental responsibility and social causes. It donates 1 percent of its sales to grassroots environmental groups, has supported various social initiatives, and consistently works toward reducing its environmental footprint. By elevating its business beyond profit, Patagonia has become a shining example of how companies can have a positive impact on the world while still being successful.

Elevating is not just about growing our businesses, though. It's about growing as individuals, as leaders, and as members of the community. How do you elevate not only your skills but also your mindset and your priorities in life? I started focusing on harmonizing, on my purpose, and on making sure that I was successful in business along with my personal life. We must continually challenge ourselves to learn, adapt, and evolve so that we can better serve those around us and create a legacy that extends beyond our own achievements.

We should not only continue to grow on our path but do so with deliberate action toward intentional results.

You can elevate by getting involved, connecting with others, and actively participating in the world around you. You can focus on creating meaningful relationships, fostering a sense of community, and inspiring others to join in your mission.

You can engage with others through mentorship. By sharing your knowledge, experiences, and guidance, you can help others grow and achieve their goals. You can also engage by participating in community events, joining industry organizations, or volunteering for causes that align with your values.

When we engage, we create a ripple effect, impacting our own lives as much as the lives of those we touch. This is how we elevate and build a legacy that truly matters, one that will continue to inspire and influence others long after we are gone.

ACTION ITEM

What is one skill, hobby, or activity you've either always wanted to do, or know that when you learn it you'll have more to offer others? When you figure that out, again, schedule it, but also schedule one more thing: the day you will pay it forward by teaching it to someone else. Remember, this is about "growing to give."

Pillar #3: Execute. How Do You Take Purposeful Action?

The third and final principle in the Legacy Factor is all about *execution*, my friend. It's about creating an enduring presence that goes from finite to infinite. Execution is about the little things that you do that make a difference.

For me, this principle hits close to home. You see, if my dad hadn't taken the position he did, our family tree would have stopped. But because he did, it has continued, and now I have two generations of Abrahams in my two granddaughters. I know that there's at least another 80 years of Abrahams on this earth. Some people might not be overjoyed by the idea of a lot of Abrahams running about, but the point is that we have to execute. We have to *do* things.

Part of executing is understanding that there has to be an effective plan in place for your future. In my life, I have a plan for my relationship, my wealth, my parenting, my grandparenting, my businesses—everything. Not because I like planning, but because I believe that we *must* have a vision. Without a vision, as they say, you shall perish. We need to have an effective plan and a visionary anticipation of what the opportunities and challenges could be so that we can execute to eliminate the challenges and promote the opportunities. In that process, you create the preparation you need to step into your full potential, to do the things that will leave an indelible, positive impact on those you touch. That's what legacy is all about.

It's truly about being prepared for both the good and the challenges as they come our way, because when we're not, we don't even recognize the opportunities. When I was told about my cancer, my life got suddenly turned upside down. The challenge I was confronting wasn't about the cancer but about what I was going to do: how I handled what I could control and responded to what I couldn't. I didn't have the luxury of not showing up, because everyone—my wife, my son, my grandchildren, my clients—was counting on me.

How do you show up when life slaps you in the face? Because it will, my friend. And it's all the work that we do up to that point that helps us prepare for it. I had to fight the cancer physically, mentally, psychologically, energetically, and medically. The tumor turned out to be seven and a half centimeters, and it took them six and a half hours to get it out. But I didn't have to fight the cancer financially because of the work that I had done to build the Legacy Factor into my financial world, into my relational world, into tomorrow. It allowed me the luxury to know that the financial side of things was taken care of. But I still needed to fight the battle, and I could fight it with the peace of mind of knowing that the people that I love and the legacy I cared about were taken care of.

I often recall this story that my friend, Les Brown, told me. It went something like this:

In a desperate situation, a young boy found himself trapped under a layer of thick ice, unable to break free. His friend, realizing the danger, tried his best to help but couldn't manage to break the ice. Frantically searching for a solution, the friend spotted a tree in the distance, broke off a large branch, and used it to pound the ice viciously. Eventually, the ice broke enough to pull his friend out just as paramedics arrived.

Astonished by the boy's incredible feat, the paramedics questioned how he found the strength to break the ice, which seemed nearly impossible.

"I know how," a nearby elderly man chimed in.

"How?" asked the paramedics.

"Because no one was around to tell him that he couldn't."

 **ACTION ITEM** Where in your life might you be listening to others or simply the voices in your head that are holding you back from moving toward something meaningful in your life? What could you do today to mute that voice and take a big step toward that meaningful goal?

PURSUE YOUR GOALS WITH A POSITIVE ATTITUDE

The power of a positive attitude can surpass expectations when we ignore the naysayers as we pursue our goals.

Take, for example, Australian entrepreneur Justin Herald. During a personal interview with him, he shared with me his remarkable story. In 1995, after being repeatedly told he had an attitude problem, Herald decided to embrace it by creating a T-shirt to sell that read, "I love my attitude." After a string of rejections from shop owners in Sydney, Herald and his friends came up with a plan where without him, they would go into stores and keep asking for Attitude Gear. After a month of this, Herald himself went back to the stores. The shop owners were begging him for his clothes by that point. It led to Herald starting his Attitude Gear clothing line, ultimately resulting in a multimillion-dollar empire.

The reality is that we either change our situation or change our results. When we are no longer able to change our situations, we are challenged to change ourselves. What changes do we need to make? It's like the mirror that Jeremy held up to me, the picture that he drew when he was five years old, that challenged me to change myself as a dad, as a business owner, as an entrepreneur, as a speaker, as an advisor, as a person. And when we do that, things shift, things change.

* * *

The Legacy Factor is about recognizing the finite time we have but also the infinite impact that we can create with the three gifts we've been given: time, talent, and treasures. To make the most of our lives, we must use these gifts wisely, invest our time in meaningful moments, and surround ourselves with supportive people.

My friends, to create a lasting legacy, we must never stop dreaming, embrace the gifts we've been given, and always pursue our goals with a positive attitude. Because your dream is coming.

CONCLUSION

Never, ever stop dreaming! Your dream is coming!

— MEL ABRAHAM

When Jeremy was 16 years old, he went away to a football camp over Father's Day weekend. While he was gone, I received an e-mail from him. Opening it, I saw a picture of a man and a boy walking at sunset on a beach with the quote from Clarence Budington Kellend that read, "He didn't tell me how to live; he lived and let me watch him do it." Jeremy had written, "Happy Father's Day. I'm sorry we're not together on Father's Day, but we'll celebrate when we get back."

It confirmed that I had done exactly what I set out to do when Jeremy was five years old. I created a life where I wasn't glued to the phones and the computer like he saw me back when I thought we were building the life we wanted. Instead, thanks to that wake-up call, I really had created the life we wanted: one we were able to spend together and take advantage of our special moments, one with fewer worries we had to deal with so we could focus on what matters the most.

As we wrap up our adventure through the Money Machine, let's take a moment to sit back and reflect on this little gem of a story about coffee cups and coffee.[1] It's a brilliant reminder of what's really important in life and how we should keep our focus on the things that matter.

So, picture this: A bunch of successful university grads swing by their old professor's place for a little catch-up session. As they chat, they start to grumble about all the hurdles and headaches that life's been throwing their way. Being the gracious host, the professor offers his guests some coffee, and he comes back with a tray loaded with all sorts of cups—china, porcelain, glass, plastic, you name it. Some are plain and simple, while others scream, "Hey, I'm fancy!" You can guess which ones the grads go for, right?

237

With a knowing smile, the professor shares a nugget of wisdom: "You see, you all beelined for the beautiful cups, didn't you? Left the plain ones all alone in the tray. Sure, it's natural to want the best for yourself, but that's exactly what's causing your stress and problems. The thing is, the cup doesn't change the quality of the coffee or make it taste any better. Most of the time, it's just pricier or even hides the true nature of the brew. You wanted the coffee, not the cup, but you couldn't help choosing the fanciest cups and then sneaking a peek at what everyone else picked."

Here's the kicker: In life, the coffee is what it's all about—our experiences and enjoyment—while the cups represent all that superficial stuff—job, money, position, and societal expectations. The cups are just tools to keep life going, but they don't dictate how awesome our lives can be. The trouble is, we sometimes get so caught up in the cups that we forget to savor the coffee.

The happiest and most fulfilled people out there? They're not the ones with the flashiest cups. They're the ones who enjoy life and make the most of what they've got. So, as you continue on your financial journey, remember to focus on the "coffee" and put your happiness and well-being front and center. Don't let the shiny "cups" distract you from what really counts—soaking up every delightful drop of life's rich brew.

The importance of creating a Money Machine cannot be overstated. It will help you create the financial freedom upon which you build your life, your relationships, and your legacy. By taking control of your finances and striving for financial liberation, you create a lasting impact that creates positive change for you today and extends far beyond your own life.

As you move forward on your wealth journey, remember the lessons you've learned and the goals you've set for yourself. Stay committed to the principles of financial literacy, and never forget the power you hold to shape your legacy and the world around you.

The power to change the financial trajectory of our lives and those of the generations to come lies within each of us. It is through our collective efforts that we can reshape the world we inhabit, creating a reality where financial success is no longer the privilege of a select few but your birthright. It's time to claim it.

Dare to dream of a world where your children and grandchildren will not be burdened by the weight of financial uncertainty but instead will inherit a legacy of prosperity and affluence. In this pursuit, you are not only securing your own financial future but also contributing to the creation of a more equitable and just society.

As you close the pages of this book, may you carry within you the burning desire to take control of your financial destiny, to break free from the chains of financial limitations, and to strive relentlessly toward the realization of your dreams. The journey to financial freedom is not one that is traveled overnight, but with each step forward, we move closer to a world where our children, and their children, will be granted the gift of a life free from the limitations of financial adversity.

Together, let us embark on this journey, charting a new course for those yet to come and forging a daily legacy that will stand the test of time. In the pursuit of financial freedom, you are not just chasing a distant dream, but rather, you are sowing the seeds of hope, opportunity, and prosperity, the fruits of which will be enjoyed by future generations.

May this book serve as the catalyst for change, inspiring you to take the reins of your financial future and to champion a new era of generational wealth and affluence. Together, we can create a brighter future for ourselves, our families, and generations to come.

Cheers to your financial freedom and creating a life that outlives you!

APPENDIX A

Financial Success Behaviors

Here are the most crucial behaviors that lay the groundwork for financial success. When consistently practiced, these behaviors will help you build a robust foundation for wealth creation and management.

1. FINANCIAL EDUCATION AND LEARNING

Embrace continuous learning and financial education as vital behaviors for achieving financial success. Stay informed about economic trends, investment strategies, and financial management techniques. Read books, attend seminars, and follow financial experts to expand your knowledge and stay current with the latest information.

2. GOAL SETTING AND PLANNING

Establish clear, specific, and measurable financial goals. Break down your goals into short-term, medium-term, and long-term objectives. Develop a detailed plan to achieve each goal, including the necessary steps, resources, and timelines.

3. BUDGETING AND EXPENSE MANAGEMENT

Effectively managing your income and expenses is a critical financial behavior. Create a monthly budget to track your income, expenses, and savings. Ensure you prioritize essential expenses, eliminate unnecessary spending, and allocate funds for savings and investments.

4. SAVING AND INVESTING

Cultivate a habit of saving a portion of your income regularly. Aim to save at least 20 to 25 percent of your earnings each month. Invest your savings in assets with growth potential, such as stocks, mutual funds, or real estate. Diversify your investments to spread risk and maximize returns.

5. BUILDING A PEACE OF MIND (EMERGENCY) FUND

Set aside money in an emergency fund to cover unexpected expenses or financial setbacks. Aim to save at least three to six months' worth of living expenses in a liquid, easily accessible account. I think you should ultimately work to have 9 to 18 months of expenses put away in a high-yield cash account.

6. PAYING OFF DEBT

Develop a plan to pay off any outstanding debt as quickly as possible. Prioritize high-interest debt and make extra payments whenever possible. Avoid taking on new debt, especially for nonessential expenses.

7. MONITORING AND ADJUSTING

Regularly review your financial progress, including your budget, savings, investments, and debt repayments. Adjust your plan as needed to stay on track with your financial goals. Be prepared to adapt your financial behaviors in response to changes in your circumstances or the economic environment.

8. SEEKING PROFESSIONAL ADVICE

When needed, consult with financial professionals, such as financial planners, tax advisors, or investment managers, to ensure you make informed decisions about your finances. A qualified expert can help you navigate complex financial situations and provide advice tailored for your unique circumstances.

9. LIVING WITHIN YOUR MEANS
Adopt a lifestyle that aligns with your financial capabilities. Avoid overspending or relying on credit to maintain a standard of living beyond your means. Focus on building wealth through saving, investing, and prudent financial management.

10. CULTIVATING A WEALTH MINDSET
Develop a positive attitude toward money and wealth creation. Embrace abundance, recognize opportunities, and believe in your ability to achieve financial success. A wealth mindset will help you overcome limiting beliefs and empower you to take control of your financial future.

* * *

By consistently practicing these behaviors, you will create a strong foundation for financial success. Remember, your financial future is within your control. Prioritize skill sets before assets, break through mental blocks, develop empowering habits, and create a Money Machine that leaves a lasting legacy.

APPENDIX B

The Language of Money Made Easy

The following is a glossary of some of the terms you may find in this book and on your financial journey. It isn't meant to be exhaustive, but it is meant to be helpful.

Accredited Investor: An individual allowed to trade securities that may not be registered with financial authorities. They need to qualify by satisfying at least one requirement regarding their income, net worth, and asset size:

— Net worth over $1 million, excluding primary residence (individually or with spouse or partner)

— Income over $200,000 (individually) or $300,000 (with spouse or partner) in each of the prior two years, and reasonably expects the same for the current year

— **NOTE:** There are also ways to qualify if you are an entity or have certain professional licenses or designations.

Active Fund: A fund that is actively managed by a person and their team.

Annuity: A financial product, typically offered by insurance companies, where you make an initial investment in return for a series of payments over time. It's a product often used to create a steady income stream, particularly for retirees.

Ask: The lowest price an owner of a stock is willing to accept for it.

Asset: Something you own that can reasonably be expected to produce money for you. Assets include stocks, bonds, commodities, real estate, and other investments.

Asset Allocation: To divide up the holdings in your portfolio by asset class. The idea is that different classes of assets perform opposite to each other, and you can limit some of your risks by allocating your portfolio according to the types of asset you have.

Asset Class: A group of different investments that have similar characteristics. For example, equities as a class are pieces of different businesses. Other asset classes include fixed income and real estate.

Balance Sheet: A statement showing what a company owns as well as the liabilities the company has, and stating the outstanding shareholder equity.

Bear Market: A market that is falling in price. A bear market has a downward trend, and someone who believes the market is headed for a drop is often referred to as a "bear." Bear markets can last for a few weeks or years.

Bid: The highest price a buyer is willing to pay when buying an investment. This is the price you will get as a seller.

Bid/Ask Spread: The difference between the asking price from a seller and the bid price from a buyer.

Blue Chips: Companies with a long history of good earnings, good balance sheets, and even regularly increasing dividends. These are solid companies that may not be exciting, but they're likely to provide reasonable returns over time. You might hear reporters and others refer to "blue-chip stocks."

Bond: An investment that represents what an entity owes you. Essentially, you lend money to a government or a company, and you are promised that the principal will be returned plus interest.

Book Value: What you have left over when you subtract the liabilities a company has from its assets and common-stock equity. Most of the time, book value is used as part of an evaluative measure rather than being truly related to a company's market value.

Broker: The entity that buys and sells investments on your behalf. Usually, you pay a fee for this service. In the case of an online discount broker, you often pay a flat commission per trade. Other brokers, especially if they also manage your assets as a whole, just charge a percentage of your assets each year. Schwab, Fidelity, and Vanguard are our favorite brokerages.

Bull Market: A market that is trending higher and likely to gain. If you think that the market is going to go up, you are considered a "bull." Additionally, like *bear*, the term can be applied to how you feel about an individual investment. If you are "bullish" on a specific company, it means you think the stock price will rise.

Capital Gain (or Loss): The difference between what you bought an investment for and what you sell it for. If you buy 100 shares of a stock at $10 a share (spending $1,000) and sell your shares later for $25 a share ($2,500), you have a capital gain of $1,500. A loss occurs when you sell for less than you paid. So, if you sell this stock for $5 instead ($500), you have a capital loss of $500.

Closed-End Funds: Funds that issue a specific number of shares at inception and whose price fluctuations are then based on the supply and demand of those shares, with no additional shares ever being issued from the fund.

Commodity: A physical material with market value that can be a "hard" commodity such as gold, silver, or copper, or a "soft" commodity such as coffee, oil, or cereals. The price of a commodity is subject to supply and demand.

Compounding: How money makes money. This is a core concept to wealth building *and* wealth erosion. The money you invest earns a return (interest and/or dividend). Then *that* interest/dividend earns a return. Effectively, you make money on what you've already made. This creates an exponential growth curve for your wealth if you allow it to continually grow. Compounding can work against you, though, if you are borrowing for your lifestyle. This is the interest you pay on your credit cards, loans, and other debt. Your interest paid becomes someone else's wealth. You want to be on the other side of that equation instead.

Cost Per Acquisition: The amount it costs to actually get a customer. Not all leads turn into customers, so this can be helpful to understand the cost for the customer instead of just the lead.

Cost Per Lead (CPL): A metric used to understand the cost of every lead that comes in the door. It is used to determine how much you are actually spending to get a lead.

Diversification: A portfolio characteristic that ensures you have more than one type of asset. It also means choosing to buy investments in different sectors, industries, or geographic locations.

Dividend: Income that a company sometimes offers to divide up among its shareholders. Dividends can be paid once, as a special case, or they can be paid more regularly—such as monthly, quarterly, semiannually, or annually.

Dow Jones Industrial Average: A price-weighted list of 30 blue-chip stocks. While there are only 30 companies included on the list, many people think of "the Dow" when they hear that "the stock market" gained or lost—it's often used as a gauge of the health of the stock market as a whole.

Earnings Per Lead (EPL): A metric used to understand the value of every lead that comes in the door. It is used to determine how much you are willing to spend to get a lead.

Equities: An asset class representing pieces of a company that you can buy. Also known as *stocks* or *shares*. The value of a share is influenced by a number of factors such as the company's profits, how its performance is perceived, and if people believe the company's value may increase in the future.

Exchange: A place where investments, including stocks, bonds, commodities, and other assets, are bought and sold. It's a place where brokers (buyers and sellers) and others can connect. While many exchanges started out with "trading floors," most orders these days are executed electronically.

ETF: An exchange-traded fund is a type of investment fund that trades like a stock. Investors buy and sell ETFs on the same exchanges as stock shares.

Fund Category: A way of differentiating mutual funds according to their investment objectives and principal investment features. This categorization allows investors to spread their money around in a mix of funds with a variety of risk and return characteristics.

— *Growth Fund:* A diversified portfolio of stocks that has capital appreciation as its primary goal, with little or no dividend payouts. The portfolio consists mainly of companies with above-average growth that reinvest their earnings into expansion, acquisitions, and/or research and development (R&D). Most growth funds offer higher potential capital appreciation but usually at above-average risk.

— *Value Fund:* A fund that follows a value-investing strategy—it seeks to invest in stocks that are deemed to be undervalued in price based on fundamental characteristics. Value investing is often compared with growth investing, which focuses on emerging companies with high growth prospects.

— *Blended Fund:* A type of equity mutual fund (also called a *blend fund*) that includes a mix of both value and growth stocks. These funds offer investors diversification among these popular investment styles in a single portfolio. Blend funds are a particular case of a hybrid fund.

Fund Manager: Someone whose job is to try to meet the stated objectives of the fund they manage. Usually, they aim to beat the specific index the fund is benchmarked against. This means the manager is responsible for both the long-term decisions about the fund, such as the overall strategy it will follow, and the day-to-day decisions, such as which shares to buy and sell.

Hard Assets: Physical or tangible assets that we can see, touch and feel, as opposed to intangible assets that not physical per se (i.e., intellectual property, patents, copyrights, and the like).

Hedge Fund: An alternative investment that uses pooled funds. A money manager or registered investment advisor sets up this type of structure as an LLC or a limited partnership. The manager raises money from outside investors and then invests and manages that money. Hedge funds are aimed at high-income investors. To be eligible to invest with a hedge fund, someone must be considered an accredited investor and earn at least $200,000 annually.

Holdings: A group of assets held in a portfolio.

Index: A tool used to statistically measure the progress of a group of investments that share characteristics. This can include a group of stocks, a group of bonds, or a group of other assets.

Index Fund: A type of mutual fund that allows you to buy investments that mimic the trends of an index. These are generally more passive investments with lower fees than other mutual funds.

IRA: A tax-advantaged individual retirement account. There are several types of IRAs. Anyone over 18 with a job can open an IRA for themselves. However, not everyone has access to every type of IRA.

Margin: Essentially, borrowed money used to make an investment. You can get credit from a broker to buy more than you actually have money for. The hope is that you'll make enough to repay the borrowed amount from your earnings.

Market Capitalization: The market cap of a company is figured by multiplying its current share price by the number of shares outstanding. The largest companies have market caps in the billions.

Money Market: A money market account is an interest-bearing account that usually pays a higher interest rate than a bank savings account would.

Mutual Fund: A fund managed by a professional portfolio manager that purchases securities with money pooled from individual investors. The fund can hold individual stocks or bonds. Such funds typically come with higher fees than other investments, since the account is actively managed.

Nasdaq: A U.S. exchange for buying and selling securities that's based in New York City. NASDAQ is an index of the stocks bought and sold on the Nasdaq exchange. (In case you're curious, the initials stand for the National Association of Securities Dealers Automated Quotations.)

New York Stock Exchange: One of the most famous stock exchanges. The NYSE trades stocks in companies all over the United States and even includes stocks of some international companies.

Open-End Funds: Funds that continually issue and buy back shares/units as demand requires it (unlike closed-end funds).

Orders: A command to buy or sell an investment. Orders can be placed in various ways, and the ways you place them can be an important part of your protection strategy. Some of the most often-used elements are below:

— *Market Order:* An order seeking execution of a buy or sell transaction immediately at the next available market price.

— *Limit Order:* An order seeking execution of a buy or sell transaction at a specified price or better.

— *Stop Order:* An order to buy or sell a security at the next available price if the price reaches or surpasses a designated level.

— *Trailing Stop:* An order to buy or sell a security that automatically adjusts the stop price at a fixed percent or dollar amount below or above the current market price.

— *Good Til Canceled.* This sets the order expiration date some-where in the future or until you cancel it. You can also have it expire at the end of the day.

— *Take Profit.* This sets a profit target to sell and lock in prof-its. Not all brokers allow this option.

Personal Investment Strategy: Exactly what it sounds like—your personal approach and strategy to investments. There's no single right way to invest. Learn about how investing works, and then define and execute your personal strategy.

P/E Ratio: A measurement that reflects how much you pay for each dollar that a company earns. A company often reports profits on a per-share basis. So, it might say it has earned $5 per share. If that same stock is selling for $75 a share on the market, you divide $75 by $5 to come up with a P/E ratio of 15. The higher a P/E ratio is, the more expectations there are for higher earnings.

Real Estate Investment Trust (REIT): A company that owns, oper-ates, or finances income-producing real estate. REITs provide a way for investors to earn a share of the income from real estate owner-ship without actually having to buy, manage, or finance any prop-erties themselves. This is typically done by pooling the capital of numerous investors. It's like a mutual fund for real estate.

Recession: Two consecutive quarters when a country sees negative economic activity. Usually, this is determined by a decline in gross domestic product (GDP) for two consecutive quarters.

Reinvestment: The earning from investments held within a fund that is reinvested to grow the fund and the value instead of being distributed on a regular basis. This also allows you to participate in compounding.

Registered Investment Advisor (RIA): A financial investment ad-visor that has been through certain training and agrees to abide by certain rules, including ensuring that recommendations and trades made on your behalf are in your best interest.

S&P 500: The Standard & Poor's 500 is a stock market index that tracks the value of 500 companies in the United States. It's similar to the Dow Jones but tracks more companies.

Stock: A unit that represents ownership in a company. Companies divide their ownership stakes into shares of stock, and the number of shares you purchase indicates your level of ownership in the company. You buy stock in the hopes that a company will be successful and more people will want a stake in it, so you can sell your stake later at a higher price than you paid.

Taxable Accounts: An account you can use for trading stocks, bonds, mutual funds, etc. Taxable accounts don't carry any tax advantages, so you'll be taxed on your investment income.

Tax-Advantaged Accounts: Investment accounts that come with tax advantages of some type. They let you defer or be exempt from taxes on investment income. Retirement accounts—where you can deduct contributions from your taxes, such as an individual retirement account (IRA)—fall into this category.

Trust Deed Lending: An investor loans money to a borrower for or on real property. The loan is secured by a trust deed, which is a legal document that places a lien on the property, effectively making the lender the property owner until it is paid in full. If the borrower defaults on the loan, the lender can foreclose and take the property.

White Labeling: Taking a product, service, or system you have and allowing others to put their name on it for a fee.

Yield: In dividend investing, the ratio between the stock price paid and the dividend paid. Say there's a stock trading at $100 per share with a dividend that amounts to $5 per year. You divide the $5 by $100 and turn the result into a percentage. In this case, the yield is 5 percent.

APPENDIX C

Ten Money Conversation Starters for Couples

1. If we could go on a dream vacation without worrying about the cost, where would we go? How can we create a savings plan to make that dream a reality together?

2. What are our top three financial goals as a couple, and how can we work together to achieve them?

3. If we each had to choose a superpower related to money management, what would it be, and why? How can we develop those skills together?

4. Imagine we just won a modest lottery prize. How would we allocate the winnings between saving, investing, and spending to strengthen our financial future?

5. What are our favorite frugal date ideas or activities that still allow us to have fun and enjoy each other's company without breaking the bank?

6. How can we create a fun and rewarding financial challenge or game for ourselves, like a savings race or a "no spend" month?

7. What's one money habit we each admire about the other, and how can we support and encourage each other in maintaining those habits?

8. How can we develop a shared budget that reflects our values, priorities, and individual preferences while still working toward our common financial goals?

9. What are some creative ways we can generate additional income streams or side hustles together to boost our financial progress?

10. What's the best financial advice we've ever received or read? How can we apply it to our lives as a couple to help us build wealth and financial security?

APPENDIX D

Ten Money Conversation Starters with Your Kids

FOR YOUNGER KIDS

1. What if we only had $20 to make today the best day ever? What fun stuff would you pick, and how can we make sure we don't spend too much?

2. Let's be shopping detectives! How can we find the best stuff without spending too much money?

3. What things do we really need, and what things are just nice to have? Can you think of some examples and tell me why we should buy what we need first?

4. Can you think of some ways to earn money for yourself? What kind of jobs do you think are good for kids to do?

5. Pretend you're running a lemonade stand. What would you do with the money you get? Would you save it, spend it, or use it to make your stand even better?

FOR OLDER CHILDREN

6. If you were given $100 and had to divide it between saving, spending, and giving, how would you allocate the money? Why?

7. What is a bank, and why do people use them? Let's discuss the benefits of having a savings account and how interest works.

8. If you had the chance to invest in a business or invention, what would it be, and why? How do investments help people grow their money?

9 Imagine you're responsible for managing a household budget. How would you make sure all the expenses are covered while still saving for the future?

10. What does it mean to be financially responsible? What does it mean to manage money wisely and what do good financial habits look like?

APPENDIX E

Business Insurances to Consider

If you're a business owner, an important way to protect your business, wealth, and lifestyle is to insure the risks that are insurable when it makes sense (as we discussed in a more general context in Chapter 17). You also know there are so many types of insurance out there. While you don't need all of these, I'll highlight some of the more common ones.

INSURANCE FOR EMPLOYERS

Businesses with employees are required by law to pay for certain types of insurance: workers' compensation insurance, unemployment insurance, and, depending on where the business is located, disability insurance.

— *Workers' Compensation Insurance.* Businesses with employees are required to carry workers' compensation insurance coverage through a commercial carrier, on a self-insured basis, or through the state Workers' Compensation Insurance program. Visit your state's Workers' Compensation Office for more information on your state's program. (Texas is the only state that doesn't require that a business carry this insurance—but it's a very good idea to have it, regardless!)

— *Unemployment Insurance Tax.* This is not a separate insurance policy that you have to buy. Businesses with employees are required to pay unemployment insurance taxes under certain conditions. If your business is required to pay these taxes, you must register your business with your state's workforce agency.

— *Disability Insurance.* Some states require employers to provide partial wage-replacement insurance coverage to their eligible employees for non-work-related sickness or injury. Currently, if your employees are located in any of the following states or territory, you are required to purchase disability insurance:

- California (Employment Development Department)

- Hawaii (Unemployment Insurance Division)

- New Jersey (Department of Labor and Workforce Development)

- New York (New York State Workers' Compensation Board)

- Puerto Rico (Departamento del Trabajo y Recursos Humanos/Department of Labor and Human Resources)

- Rhode Island (Rhode Island Department of Labor and Training)

OTHER BUSINESS INSURANCE

Insurance coverage is available for every conceivable risk your business might face. Cost and amount of policy coverage vary among insurers. You should discuss your specific business risks and the types of insurance available with your insurance agent or broker. Your agency can advise you on the exact types of insurance you should consider purchasing.

The following types of coverage may be important to get, depending on the type of business you own:

— *General Liability Insurance.* This is to cover any legal hassles for a business owner due to accidents, injuries, and claims of negligence. These policies protect against payments as the result of bodily injury, property damage, medical expenses, libel, slander, the cost of defending lawsuits, and settlement bonds or judgments required during an appeal procedure.

— *Product Liability Insurance.* Companies that manufacture, wholesale, distribute, and retail a product may be liable for its safety. Product liability insurance protects against financial loss as a result of a defective product that causes injury or bodily harm. The amount of insurance you should purchase depends on the products you sell or manufacture. A clothing store would have far less risk than a small appliance store, for example.

— *Professional Liability Insurance.* Business owners providing services should consider having professional liability insurance (also known as errors and omissions insurance). This type of liability coverage protects your business against malpractice, errors, and negligence in provision of services to your customers. Depending on your profession, you may be required by your state government to carry such a policy. For example, physicians are required to purchase malpractice insurance as a condition of practicing in certain states.

— *Home-Based Business Insurance.* Contrary to popular belief, homeowners' insurance policies do not generally cover home-based business losses. Depending on risks to your business, you may add riders to your homeowners' policy to cover normal business risks such as property damage. However, homeowners' policies only go so far in covering home-based businesses, and you may need to purchase additional policies to cover other risks, such as general and professional liability.

— *Commercial Property Insurance.* Property insurance covers everything related to the loss and damage of company property due to a wide variety of events such as fire, smoke, windstorms and hailstorms, civil disobedience, and vandalism. The definition of *property* is broad and includes lost income, business interruption, buildings, computers, company papers, and money.

Property insurance policies come in two basic forms: (1) all-risk policies covering a wide range of incidents and perils except those noted in the policy; (2) peril-specific policies that cover losses from only those perils listed in the policy.

Examples of peril-specific policies include fire, flood, crime, and business-interruption insurance. All-risk policies generally cover risks faced by the average small business, while peril-specific policies are usually purchased when there is high risk of peril in a certain area. Consult your insurance agent or broker about the type of business property insurance best suited for your small business.

DISABILITY INSURANCE

In addition to the types of insurance above, disability insurance can be vital not just to protect you in times of emergencies, but to protect your business as well. Choosing insurance is a great way to ease difficult situations you may encounter. Out of the various types of disability insurance policies you can choose from, here are five:

— *Individual Disability Insurance.* This insurance is made for the self-employed or for employees with no company insurance. The benefits and premiums may differ depending on the need of the individual with regard to the kind of work, the risk involved, and the state the insured resides in. Higher premiums are applied to policies that have wider coverage for a broad category of circumstances.

— *Business Overhead Expense Disability Insurance.* Business overhead expense disability insurance is intended to offer funds for the overhead expenses incurred in case the owner suffers a disability. This insurance can help the owner with business-related expenses such as rent or mortgage costs and maintenance fees.

— *Key-Person Disability Insurance.* When a key person in a business becomes disabled, this insurance can give the business owner the benefits of continuing with the business transactions that the key person has left behind. This enables the business to move forward and go on without losing profit.

— *High-Limit Disability Insurance.* This policy entitles the insured to a 65 percent income-replacement benefit regardless of income level. This disability insurance is on top of a coverage that is already in force.

— *Employer-Supplied Disability Insurance.* As one may get injured on a job, the employer acquires this insurance for the employees. Under this policy is the workers' compensation. It's important to note that this insurance is only valid when the employee is hurt while working.

ENDNOTES

Introduction

1. "Stress in America 2022: Concerned for the Future, Beset by Inflation," American Psychological Association, October 2022, https://www.apa.org/news /press/releases/stress/2022/concerned-future-inflation.

Chapter 1

1. "Stress in America 2022: Concerned for the Future, Beset by Inflation," American Psychological Association, October 2022, https://www.apa.org/news /press/releases/stress/2022/concerned-future-inflation.

2. Ramsey Solutions, *The National Study of Millionaires*, April 12, 2023, https://www .ramseysolutions.com/retirement/the-national-study-of-millionaires-research.

Chapter 2

1. "Majority of Americans on $100,000 Salaries Are Living Paycheck to Paycheck," FOX 5 New York, February 2, 2023, https://www.fox5ny.com/news/americans -living-paycheck-to-paycheck-100k.

2. Ramsey Solutions, *The National Study of Millionaires*, April 12, 2023, https://www .ramseysolutions.com/retirement/the-national-study-of-millionaires-research.

3. Ramsey Solutions, *National Study of Millionaires*.

Chapter 4

1. Donnelly et al., "The Amount and Source of Millionaires' Wealth (Moderately) Predict Their Happiness," *Personality and Social Psychology Bulletin* 44, no. 5 (May 2018): 684–99. https://doi.org/10.1177/0146167217744766.

Chapter 5

1. Moriah Costa, "What's the Median Retirement Savings by Age?," Synchrony Bank (blog), September 8, 2023, https://www.synchronybank.com/blog/median -retirement-savings-by-age/.

2. "How to Plan for Rising Health Care Costs," Fidelity Viewpoints, https://www .fidelity.com/viewpoints/personal-finance/plan-for-rising-health-care-costs.

Chapter 9

1. Julia Kagan, "What Is the 4% Rule for Withdrawals in Retirement and How Much Can You Spend?," Investopedia, last modified January 20, 2022, https://www.investopedia.com/terms/f/four-percent-rule.asp.

Chapter 10

1. Wendy Wood, Jeffrey M. Quinn, and Deborah A. Kashy, "Habits in Everyday Life: Thought, Emotion, and Action," *Journal of Personality and Social Psychology* 83, no. 6 (December 2002): 1281–97, https://pubmed.ncbi.nlm.nih.gov/12500811/.

Chapter 11

1. Anthony P. Carnevale, Stephen J. Rose, and Ban Cheah, *The College Payoff: Education, Occupations, Lifetime Earnings*, Georgetown University Center on Education and the Workforce, 2011, https://cew.georgetown.edu/wp-content/uploads/collegepayoff-completed.pdf.

2. Stephen Miller, "Educational Assistance Programs Lead to Career Success," SHRM, November 2, 2015, https://www.shrm.org/resourcesandtools/hr-topics/benefits/pages/educational-assistance.aspx.

Chapter 12

1. Lane Gillespie, *Bankrate's 2024 Annual Emergency Savings Report*, Bankrate, January 24, 2024, https://www.bankrate.com/banking/savings/emergency-savings-report/.

Chapter 14

1. Ramsey Solutions, *The National Study of Millionaires*, April 12, 2023, https://www.ramseysolutions.com/retirement/the-national-study-of-millionaires-research.

Chapter 17

1. "70% of Rich Families Lose Their Wealth by the Second Generation," Money.com, June 17, 2015, https://money.com/rich-families-lose-wealth/

2. "2017 Commissioners Standard Ordinary (CSO) Tables," Society of Actuaries, n.d., https://www.soa.org/resources/experience-studies/2015/2017-cso-tables/.

Chapter 18

1. Hanna Horvath and Jenn Jones, "Can Medical Bankruptcy Help with Medical Bills?" *USA Today*, November 13, 2023, https://www.usatoday.com/money/blueprint/debt/can-medical-bankruptcy-help-with-medical-bills.

2. Angela Leicht, "When Should You Buy Long-Term Care Insurance?" *CBS News*, September 26, 2023, https://www.cbsnews.com/news/when-should-you-buy-long-term-care-insurance.

3. "Cost of Care Survey," Genworth, June 2, 2022, https://www.genworth.com/aging-and-you/finances/cost-of-care.html.

Chapter 21

1. "How a Rejected Block of Marble Became the World's Most Famous Statue," Brittanica.com, accessed January 29, 2024, https://www.britannica.com/story/how-a-rejected-block-of-marble-became-the-worlds-most-famous-statue.

2. IBM Institute for Business Value, "Sustainability at a Turning Point: Consumers Are Pushing Companies to Pivot," IBM.com, May 2021, https://www.ibm.com/downloads/cas/WLJ7LVP4.

Conclusion

1. Munna Prawin, "Life Is Like a Cup of Coffee," *Thoughts to Inspire* (blog), June 4, 2012, https://munnaprawin.com/2012/06/04/life-is-like-a-cup-of-coffee/.

ACKNOWLEDGMENTS

From the concept to the completed manuscript, this book took 75 days of dedication from a lot of people. As I always say, there is no such thing as "self-made." This book is no different. It's been made possible by the many beautiful souls who believed in me, supported me, and pushed me to serve at a higher level. Nothing I say will do justice to the level of respect, gratitude, and love I have for each of you. You truly have brought richness to my life.

Let me start with my brother from another mother, Brendon Burchard. You've been with me every step of the way, and most of what I do today is because you pushed me to grow and gave me the ability to grow my wings. We've been on this road together for over a decade and a half, and I feel we're just hitting our stride. Thank you to you and your wonderful wife, Denise, for being such shining beacons in my life.

My Laguna neighbor (who moved away), James Wedmore: you were the one who showed me that I needed to see my work through the eyes of service and a new calling. You've openly shared your platforms, stages, and friendship in such a way that I would not be here today without them. Although you've opted for the mountains of Sedona versus the beaches of Laguna, my friend, know that your impact is felt and appreciated each and every day. May we get older but never lose the childlike playfulness that fuels us.

OMG, then there is Jenni Robbins. You've seen me through all the journeys since we met more than 15 years ago. You are wise beyond your years, and I have been the beneficiary of that sacred gift. Your friendship is one of the greatest blessings this journey has gifted me. Thank you.

My friend Brandon Lucero: as much as I always knew that words mattered, you helped me refine the ones I use and to touch the hearts and souls of those I serve. You rock, my friend, and I am truly grateful.

Also, Lauren Eckhardt, who saw my vision more as a move-ment toward freedom than simply a book to be written, and helped me create this from the first word. We toiled over the man-uscript together, and you became the voice of my audience in the process. You spent endless hours letting me rant, speak, and write this book, and then you dug in further to find even more gold to add to these pages. The book would not be what it is without your hand and heart in it.

To all my Napa Gang and GrowthDay brothers and sisters: thank you, Brendon, for bringing me into the family. You all have inspired me to be more than I am, to serve for more than the moment, and to give with grace no matter the circumstance.

I am profoundly grateful to Hay House for their belief, trust, and willingness to get behind this vision. From the moment Amy Kiberd contacted me, she saw the power of the work and cham-pioned it to Reid Tracy and Patty Gift. Not only did they see the vision, they got behind it in a big way with a dedicated team, including Lisa Cheng, Monica O'Connor, and Nicolette Salamanca Young spearheading a hugely compressed timeline to bring this to life. Without your belief, trust, and diligence, none of this would have happened.

I could not write this without acknowledging you, the reader; my audience; and every person I ever had the blessing to speak in front of, coach, serve, or simply have a conversation with. Y'all are the fuel for why I do what I do. Just knowing that I might change one life is enough to keep me on this road, serving you.

Now, my family: you are my North Star and what keeps me so invested in this journey of life, to live it fully expressed and immersed. Without you, none of this has any meaning.

To my amazing wife and partner in life, Stefanie: you cap-tured my heart 14 years ago, yet you've shown me that love is forever expanding. You brought grace to my cancer journey that I would've never imagined having if it weren't for you. You fill my soul daily with your beauty, support, and love. You humor me when my humor and shenanigans make no sense to you. There is no one I want on this journey with me other than you. I love you, my beautiful wife.

My incredible son, Jeremy: you are one of my life's greatest gifts and one of my life's greatest teachers. Much of what I've done is because I knew you were watching, and I didn't want to mess up. In the early years, you were the thing that was worth fighting for. Seeing the man you've become, the husband to Kamie, and now father to our two precious granddaughters, Emily and Aria, defines what the Legacy Factor is all about. Your wonderful wife is such a gift to us. She too, is an amazing spirit, a financial professional in her own right, and a wonderful wife and mother who embodies the core of this book. The two of you are not only much of why this book was written, but whom it was written for.

My brother, Jeff: you were always the wind beneath my wings. You've been the catalyst for me to go after my dreams. I couldn't ask for a better brother or friend who, without knowing it, pushed me to be better.

To Mom, for always being the pillar of strength in our family. You and Dad taught us kids that if we have the ability, it is our responsibility to make a difference and help others.

My cousin who is more like a brother, Richard Ardi: where do I start—you were my first client when I started on my own, and you took great joy in testing me and what I stood for. You set the stage for me to become who I am, not only financially, but as a man. Thanks for always being there in your uniquely irritating but loving way.

I am humbled by knowing each of you and being loved by you. Thank you for being a part of this incredible journey.

With heartfelt gratitude,
Mel

ABOUT THE AUTHOR

Mel Abraham, a visionary financial expert, author, speaker, and entrepreneur, is the guiding light for countless entrepreneurs seeking to transform their lives and build their dreams. As the founder of the Affluence Blueprint™ and Thoughtpreneur Academy, Mel's unwavering dedication to empowering individuals and their businesses has earned him a reputation as one of the most sought-after financial and strategic business mentors of our time.

In his first book, a number-one bestseller, *The Entrepreneur's Solution: The Modern Millionaire's Path to More Profit, Fans & Freedom*, Mel shares the culmination of his experiences and insights, inspiring readers to embark on their own entrepreneurial journey.

Mel's life took an unexpected turn when he discovered a cancerous tumor in his bladder in June 2019. This harrowing experience only strengthened his resolve to share his Affluence Blueprint and the Legacy Factor with the world. His teachings now center on empowering others to close the gap between their current situation and their true potential, creating lives that are deeply valued, impactful, and imbued with a sense of financial freedom.

With a heart full of wisdom and a spirit brimming with passion, Mel has become the Affluence Mentor™ and the "thought leader to thought leaders," guiding some of the greatest minds of our time in business, finance, and personal development.

Having lived through the exhilarating highs and heart-wrenching lows of building, buying, and selling numerous multimillion-dollar businesses for himself and his clients, Mel's strategies have become a beacon of hope for thousands of people across the globe. His belief in the entrepreneurial way of life is grounded in the notion that everyone, regardless of their circumstances, can manifest a life of abundance, meaning, and purpose.

Through his work, Mel aspires to ignite the financial-freedom spirit within all who cross his path, transforming society from a state of mere existence to one where individuals can embrace life on their own terms, living boldly and passionately.

Mel is a CPA by education but an entrepreneur by exhilaration and sees his calling in this new season of his life to be the bright light of hope and possibility for those who know there's something more for them but are unsure of how to get there.

When Mel isn't inspiring others through speaking, training, or mentoring, he can be found working out, training in martial arts, or creating unforgettable memories with his beautiful wife, Stefanie, and their Sheepadoodles, Budo and Samson. Together, they explore exotic locales and cherish the simple pleasures of life, such as relaxing at the beach that they call home.

To learn more about Mel and his work or to book him to speak, visit his website at **www.MelAbraham.com** and connect with him on:

Facebook: melhabraham

Instagram: @melabraham9

YouTube: @MelHAbraham

Podcast: TheAffluentEntrepreneurShow.com

X: @MelHAbraham

LinkedIn: melhabraham

Hay House Titles of Related Interest

THE SHIFT, the movie,
starring Dr. Wayne W. Dyer
(available as an online streaming video)
Learn more at www.hayhouse.com/the-shift-movie

***

HIGH PERFORMANCE HABITS: How Extraordinary People Become That Way, by Brendon Burchard

MILLIONAIRE SUCCESS HABITS: The Gateway to Wealth & Prosperity, by Dean Graziosi

TWO WEEKS NOTICE: Find the Courage to Quit Your Job, Make More Money, Work Where You Want, and Change the World, by Amy Porterfield

WHAT'S IN IT FOR THEM?: 9 Genius Networking Principles to Get What You Want by Helping Others Get What They Want, by Joe Polish

All of the above are available at your local bookstore or may be ordered by visiting:

Hay House USA: www.hayhouse.com®
Hay House Australia: www.hayhouse.com.au
Hay House UK: www.hayhouse.co.uk
Hay House India: www.hayhouse.co.in

***

We hope you enjoyed this Hay House book. If you'd like to receive our online catalog featuring additional information on Hay House books and products, or if you'd like to find out more about the Hay Foundation, please contact:

Hay House LLC, P.O. Box 5100, Carlsbad, CA 92018-5100
(760) 431-7695 or (800) 654-5126
www.hayhouse.com® • www.hayfoundation.org

———

Published in Australia by:
Hay House Australia Publishing Pty Ltd
18/36 Ralph St., Alexandria NSW 2015
Phone: +61 (02) 9669 4299
www.hayhouse.com.au

Published in the United Kingdom by:
Hay House UK Ltd
The Sixth Floor, Watson House,
54 Baker Street, London W1U 7BU
Phone: +44 (0) 203 927 7290
www.hayhouse.co.uk

Published in India by:
Hay House Publishers (India) Pvt Ltd
Muskaan Complex, Plot No. 3,
B-2, Vasant Kunj, New Delhi 110 070
Phone: +91 11 41761620
www.hayhouse.co.in

———

Access New Knowledge.
Anytime. Anywhere.

Learn and evolve at your own pace
with the world's leading experts.

www.hayhouseU.com